'As a parent of a SEN child, I've known how wonderful it can be but also how much help we need…this book is fun, interactive AND educational – great reading for parents like us!'
– Carol Vorderman MBE, broadcaster and educator

'This book is a genuinely wonderful resource. Parenting is a daunting task for anyone, particularly if you have a child with special educational needs. Georgina Durrant, through her years as a teacher (and mum!), has developed a wide assortment of activities to engage your child in ways that are rewarding and effective and above all, FUN. Use this book!'
– Rob Delaney, BAFTA winning co-creator and star
of Channel 4's *Catastrophe*

'Georgina Durrant has created a simple and adaptable resource that highlights the value of play and the array of skills that can be developed within it. With activities for inside and out, there's something to suit everyone, whatever the weather!'
– Elaine Scougal, SEN parent/blogger, Dundee

'It's been so tough for children during the pandemic, not being able to see friends and just play with them. But playing is also key to building thriving brains, bodies, and social bonds – all important in today's world. Research shows play can improve children's abilities to plan, organise, get along with others, and regulate emotions. Play also helps with language, maths and social skills, and even helps children cope with stress. So, I can't recommend Georgina Durrant's *100 Ways Your Child Can Learn Through Play* highly enough. It's bursting with fun activities to do in the garden, on a walk, sitting still or on a rainy day. Your kids will love it and you'll be taking care of their mental health at this difficult time too while having LOADS of fun!'
– Sue Atkins BBC, Disney and ITV *This Morning* **parenting expert and**
author of *The Can Do Kid's Journal: Discover your Confidence Superpower!*

'At last, a timely and relevant life-saver of a book by someone who "gets it"! *100 Ways Your Child Can Learn Through Play* contains enriching activities to appeal to every child and busy parent, regardless of need. Not only are they cheap and simple for busy parents to incorporate into their daily routines, but the focus is very much on fun which for me is the best way to connect with my girls, particularly during these difficult times.'
– Hayley Newman, blogger and speaker at Downs Side Up

'What an utterly fantastic book this is! Practical ideas for play which feel very manageable even if play doesn't come naturally to you or you don't have access to endless space or resources. As soon as I started reading I couldn't wait to start playing.'
– Dr Pooky Knightsmith, child and adolescent mental health expert

of related interest

Promoting Young Children's Emotional Health and Wellbeing
A Practical Guide for Professionals and Parents
Sonia Mainstone-Cotton
ISBN 978 1 78592 054 7
eISBN 978 1 78450 311 6

Creative Coping Skills for Children
Emotional Support through Arts and Crafts Activities
Bonnie Thomas
ISBN 978 1 84310 921 1
eISBN 978 1 84642 954 5

Building Positive Momentum for Positive Behavior in Young Children
Strategies for Success in School and Beyond
Lisa Rogers
ISBN 978 1 78592 774 4
eISBN 978 1 78450 679 7

100 WAYS

Your Child Can Learn

THROUGH PLAY

· · · · · · · · · · ·

Fun Activities for Young Children with SEN

Georgina Durrant

ILLUSTRATED BY CHRISTOPHER BARNES

Jessica Kingsley Publishers
London and Philadelphia

First published in Great Britain in 2021
by Jessica Kingsley Publishers
An Hachette Company

1

Copyright © Georgina Durrant 2021
Illustrations copyright © Christopher Barnes 2021

Disclaimer: images shown are for illustration purposes only and may not be an exact representation of the activities.

A CIP catalogue record for this title is available from the British Library and the Library of Congress

ISBN 978 1 78775 734 9
eISBN 978 1 78775 735 6

Printed and bound in Great Britain by Bell & Bain Ltd

Jessica Kingsley Publishers' policy is to use papers that are natural, renewable and recyclable products and made from wood grown in sustainable forests. The logging and manufacturing processes are expected to conform to the environmental regulations of the country of origin.

Jessica Kingsley Publishers
Carmelite House
50 Victoria Embankment
London EC4Y 0DZ

www.jkp.com

Dedicated to my children,
for reminding me of the importance of play.

ACKNOWLEDGMENTS

I'd like to thank Jessica Kingsley Publishers for saying 'yes' to my book proposal, despite it being pitched at the start of a global pandemic! Thanks, in particular, to my editor Emily, for always being on hand to answer my questions.

A huge thank you to everyone who follows my blog, The SEN Resources Blog, for reading my posts and sharing them. You all helped me get to a point where I was able to approach a publisher with my book idea.

Thank you to my husband and family for helping me to carve out some time in our busy lives for me to write this book and for being my biggest supporters.

I would also like to thank my parents, who brought me up in a household full of fun, play and love that no doubt influenced my view on the importance of play.

And a huge thank you to my brother and best friend, the most talented artist I know, who agreed to draw all one hundred images for my book just because I phoned and asked him.

CONTENTS

Chapter 3: Sitting Still 51

Chapter 4: Rainy Day Play 69

Chapter 5: Crafts 87

Chapter 6: Sensory Play 105

PREFACE

· · · · · · · · · · · · · · · · · · · ·

Whether it's raining and you're stuck inside, your child is overstimulated and needs some sensory play or you're off on a train journey and need ideas to keep your child engaged while sat still, this book is designed to give you one hundred ways to keep your child entertained. What's more, I've sneaked into each activity lots of skill-based learning, so while your child is happy playing or creating, you can sit there confident in the knowledge that they are also developing a whole array of skills through play.

I also wanted this book to help you if you're feeling a bit overwhelmed with how best to develop certain skills with your child. It's all well and good being told by your child's school that they need to improve their motor skills, or communication skills, but how do you do this? Where do you start? What can you do at home or out and about with your child to develop these skills? At the bottom of each activity, you'll find a handy 'skills' box highlighting the skills that the activity can help your child develop. For example, if you're looking for some ways to improve their working memory, you can easily scan through the pages to find activities that have the working memory box ticked.

I hope that my book is used as a sort of 'play recipe book', which you can get down from the shelf, prop up on your kitchen table and look through with your child to decide what you're going to do today. As you would with recipes, I'd also like you to experiment with it. If one of the activities doesn't quite suit your child, amend it, just like you would if there's an ingredient in a cake recipe that your child dislikes or you haven't got in your cupboard. I've added suggestions for ways you can extend and adapt each activity but feel empowered that you are the expert on your child, and you will know the best way to make these activities work for your family. It may be that your child has a visual impairment, for example, and the activity is to look for coloured objects, so you could choose to adapt it to find items of different textures instead. Or if your child has colour-blindness, for this activity you could choose the colours that they can differentiate between.

You may be wondering why all the activities are play based. Simply, it's because I'm a huge believer in the importance of play and, I would argue, so are children! In my experience as a teacher, special educational needs and disabilities coordinator (SENDCO), mum and author of The SEN Resources Blog, play is the most wonderful way to learn! In my opinion, children learn more when they are happy and having fun. Therefore, all the activities in this book have fun at the very centre of them, with lots of learning skills intertwined.

In case you're wondering who I am and why I've written this book, I'm Georgina. I'm a mum of two and a former teacher/SENDCO. I now run the popular website, The SEN Resources Blog, a site for parents and teachers of children with special educational needs (SEN). It started off as just a way for me to share my ideas for activities and to recommend some resources. It's now become one of the most popular SEN websites in the UK. I decided to write this book because I wanted to share my ideas with even more families. I really hope after reading it that you feel more confident that your child is learning through play and that you will have fun together with these activities.

Here's what you can expect in each chapter:

Chapter 1 – In the Garden

Chapter 1 is all about ways your child can learn through play in the garden or an outside space. I've witnessed how some children become a bit 'lost' when playing outside. They may love being outside, but without the structure of activities they quickly become overwhelmed and unsure what to do when left to their own devices. That's where this chapter comes in handy. With this book in your hands you've now got almost 20 activities designed just for the garden/outside space. From digging for pretend dinosaurs to going on a barefoot sensory walk around the garden, you'll have plenty of ways to keep them learning through play outside.

Chapter 2 – On a Walk

I'm sure I can't be the only one who, while on a walk, regularly hears from my kids comments like, 'My legs are tired', 'I'm hungry', 'It's too far"! This chapter is bursting with games, nature hunts and silly challenges to help make your walks even more fun and, I hope, distract your children from the length of the walk!

Chapter 3 – Sitting Still

This chapter arms you with play-based learning activities for those tricky situations when your child needs to sit still for a period of time. I hope that if and when you're anxious about long journeys, or having to keep your child relatively still at a wedding, you can pop this book in your bag and whip it out, knowing that there's a whole chapter's worth of activities to help you!

Chapter 4 – Rainy Day Imaginative Play

This is a collection of different role-play and small-world play activities that you can play together to develop key skills. I appreciate that imaginative play can be difficult for some children, with it often being seen as open-ended play, so I've tried some structure to it to make it more accessible. I've often found that imaginative play activities can be fantastic for developing social skills, role-playing life skills and developing language and communication skills. These activities are not just about developing verbal communication – if your child uses sign language or visuals to communicate, use these activities to help them practise these.

Chapter 5 – Crafts

Crafts are absolutely fantastic for developing a whole range of skills but like Marmite, children either love them or hate them. Some children will happily sit making and creating while others might prefer to run around and resist the idea of doing a craft together. In my experience, some children dislike crafts because the activity is far too unstructured; they are sat with an array of craft materials and don't know where to begin, so 'switch off' from the activity. Another reason is that they think they aren't very good at it. Therefore, these craft activities have lots of structure and purpose in them. They are short and snappy, with set instructions and achievable end goals.

Chapter 6 – Sensory Play

Perhaps the most useful chapter in the whole book, this is full of sensory play activities. Sensory play stimulates a child's senses and for many children is a wonderful way to help them feel relaxed. If your child has had a busy day or has struggled with their emotions, you can flick to this chapter and try out a few of these activities to see if it helps them to regulate their emotions and find calm. These can be particularly useful to do in the evening, helping your child to relax before attempting bedtime.

Throughout the book, I refer to a collection of skills that the activities may help to develop. These are explained below:

Language and communication – The activities that tick this box will be the ones that help children to practise either verbal communication or communication through sign language or visuals.

Literacy/Numeracy – These are the activities in the book that develop your child's reading and writing or their maths skills.

Concentration – Any of the activities that require your child to focus for a period of time will help to develop this skill.

Social skills – These are the skills that are needed in social situations. Examples include taking turns, learning to lose or win gracefully and working as a team.

Problem-solving – Activities that will tick this box will be those that require your child to analyse a situation and find a solution themselves.

Motor skills – These include fine and gross motor skills. Fine motor skill activities are those that develop the tiny muscles in the fingers and hands that are needed to learn to write and complete other tasks such as using a zip when getting dressed. Gross motor skills are those that use the bigger muscles. Activities such as jumping or throwing use gross motor skills.

Emotional regulation – This is the skill of managing their own emotions. This could be learning ways that help them feel calm when they are feeling overstimulated.

Sensory integration – These are the tasks that will require your child to learn to process and organize sensory information (touch, sight, sounds, smells, taste, body position and movement) to carry out an activity.

Working memory – These activities require a child to remember information, perhaps in an order, for a short amount of time in order to successfully carry out the task.

CHAPTER 1

IN THE GARDEN

1. DINOSAUR FOSSIL SAND DIG

Description
Transport little ones into the world of palaeontology by inviting them to take part in their very own 'fossil' dig. This is a fantastic way of giving purpose to sand play while developing fine motor skills and concentration.

Equipment
Sand (designed for a sand pit), sand pit/tray, toy dinosaurs or fossils, paintbrushes, spatulas and tweezers.

How to
1. Bury their pretend dinosaur fossils or toy dinosaurs under some sand in either your sand pit or a tray.
2. Provide your child with various equipment to carefully excavate the 'fossils'.
3. Let your child enjoy digging for fossils and brushing the sand off their prehistoric discoveries!

Alternatives
Change the sand for other mediums such as oats or dried pasta.

Extras
In Chapter 6 (activity 82) I show you how to make fossils using salt dough. These could be used instead of dinosaur fossils/toys for this activity.

Parent/Carer tips
Carefully removing the sand from the 'fossils' using paintbrushes is great for practising fine motor skills, especially if you encourage them to be careful and pretend the fossils are delicate specimens! Using tweezers to pick up the 'fossils' is an excellent way of developing hand strength.

SKILLS

☐ Language & communication	☐ Social skills	☐ Emotional regulation
☐ Literacy/Numeracy	☑ Problem-solving	☑ Sensory integration
☑ Concentration	☑ Motor skills	☐ Working memory

2. LETTER SPRAY

Description

This is a fun-filled, water play activity to encourage children to learn the letters of the alphabet by squirting them with water! It is easily adaptable for learning phonics too.

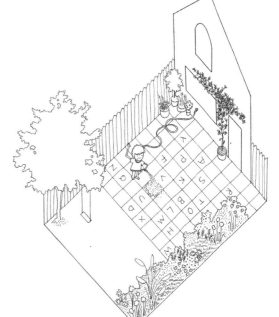

Equipment

Chalk and a water pistol/hosepipe.

How to

1. Write the letters of the alphabet on a fence or paving stones in a jumbled order.
2. Fill your child's water pistol with water.
3. Shout out a letter and ask your child to find the letter and squirt it with water to make it 'magically' disappear!
4. Take it in turns to shout out the letters and squirt them.

Alternatives

Write the numbers 1–10 instead of letters, to help develop your child's number recognition skills.

Extras

For children learning phase 2 phonics and beyond, you could swap the letters for digraphs and trigraphs – for example, 'sh' and 'igh'.

Parent/Carer tips

It may be best to start with just a few letters initially before making it more challenging, in order to keep this fun and build your child's confidence.

SKILLS

☑ Language & communication	☑ Social skills	☐ Emotional regulation
☑ Literacy/Numeracy	☐ Problem-solving	☐ Sensory integration
☐ Concentration	☑ Motor skills	☑ Working memory

3. BEAN BAG NUMBER AIM

Description
Develop children's gross motor skills while practising basic maths in this active challenge. This is fantastic for perfecting number recognition skills.

Equipment
Chalk, bean bags (or similar), paving stones/concrete and card (optional extra).

How to
1. Draw five large circles on the paving stones using chalk.
2. Write a different number inside each circle.
3. Shout out a number and challenge your child to find the correct circle to aim for and throw their bean bag into.

Alternatives
Change it to practise letters or shapes.

Extras
Challenge your child's hand–eye coordination, concentration and accuracy by making the circles smaller or further away.

Parent/Carer tips
Encourage your child to take turns to throw or call out the numbers to help them develop their language and communication skills as well as the social skill of turn-taking.

SKILLS

☑ Language & communication	☑ Social skills	☐ Emotional regulation
☑ Literacy/Numeracy	☐ Problem-solving	☐ Sensory integration
☑ Concentration	☑ Motor skills	☑ Working memory

4. CEREAL BIRD FEEDER

Description

Perhaps the easiest way to make a beautiful bird feeder for your garden, while also developing your child's fine motor skills and hand–eye coordination.

Equipment

Cereal hoops and pipe cleaners.

How to

1. Bend one end of the pipe cleaner back on itself and twist.
2. Encourage your child to thread the cereal hoops onto the pipe cleaner, leaving a few centimetres of the pipe cleaner at the end.
3. Twist the ends together and bend the left-over pipe cleaner end into a loop to hook onto a tree branch or a nail to hang it in the garden.
4. Enjoy watching the birds eat the cereal hoops off it.

Alternatives

If you don't have pipe cleaners, you can use string or ribbon.

Extras

Your child could make the bird feeder into different shapes.

Parent/Carer tips

Make sure to remove this bird feeder if it's not eaten by the birds, to avoid it growing mould. If possible, use a lower-sugar cereal for the health of the birds.

SKILLS

☐ Language & communication	☐ Social skills	☐ Emotional regulation
☐ Literacy/Numeracy	☑ Problem-solving	☐ Sensory integration
☑ Concentration	☑ Motor skills	☑ Working memory

5. TOY CAR WASH

Description

Provide a purpose to your child's water play by helping them to pretend that they are running a car wash for their toy cars. Sparkling clean toys may be the added bonus of this activity!

Equipment

Soap, water, sponges, brushes, towels and plastic toy cars (non-electrical).

How to

1. Provide your child with equipment such as brushes, sponges, soap and water.
2. Support your child in washing their toys.
3. Provide your child with towels to dry their toys afterwards.

Alternatives

Create a baby doll bath set-up instead, where your child can practise taking care of their doll by washing it carefully.

Extras

Set this up to look like a real car wash, complete with a sign, queue of toy vehicles and toy people.

Parent/Carer tips

Pretend play can be fantastic for a child's language and communication skills. Children often practise these skills without realizing during pretend play, sometimes talking to (or acting as) the toys.

SKILLS

☑ Language & communication	☑ Social skills	☐ Emotional regulation
☐ Literacy/Numeracy	☑ Problem-solving	☐ Sensory integration
☑ Concentration	☑ Motor skills	☑ Working memory

6. COLOURFUL BUBBLE SOCK

Description
Let your child enjoy the ultimate homemade bubble-blowing experience by making their very own bubble sock. This can be a wonderful sensory experience for children, especially if they are feeling overstimulated.

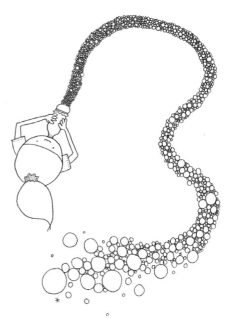

Equipment
Old sock, plastic bottle, scissors, elastic band, water, washing-up liquid, plastic bowl and food colouring (optional).

How to
1. Cut the base off a plastic bottle using scissors and discard it.
2. Help your child to put the sock over the open end of the bottle and secure it with an elastic band.
3. Put washing-up liquid and water into a plastic bowl.
4. Dip the end with the sock attached, into the soap and water mix.
5. Show your child how blowing from the other end to the sock creates a long length of bubbles all attached together. Let them have a go!

Alternatives
Use a tennis racket to dip into a bucket full of washing-up liquid and water, then wave it around to create lots of small bubbles.

Extras
Make it colourful by adding food colouring to the end of the sock. Beware that some food colouring may stain clothing and surfaces.

Parent/Carer tips
An adult will need to cut the plastic bottle. Make your child aware that the cut end of the bottle can be sharp.

SKILLS
☐ Language & communication	☐ Social skills	☑ Emotional regulation
☐ Literacy/Numeracy	☑ Problem-solving	☑ Sensory integration
☐ Concentration	☑ Motor skills	☑ Working memory

7. PIRATE TREASURE HUNT

Description

Hide some pretend 'treasure' in the garden and create your very own map for your child to use to find it! This is a brilliant, fun, imaginative play activity.

Equipment

'Treasure' (this could be a plastic toy), paper and pens.

How to

1. Create a simple map, showing the key 'landmarks' of your garden, such as the bird table, gate, bushes and flowerpots. Hide the treasure and draw an 'X' on the map where it is hidden.
2. Give your child the map, discuss with them what the pictures are of, helping them to get their bearings. Set the scene of them being a pirate and their mission is to find the hidden treasure.
3. Support them to look for the treasure, perhaps giving them clues if needed.

Alternatives

Although this is designed to be an outdoor activity, it can easily be done inside too.

Extras

Your child could try creating their own map and hiding the treasure themselves. To make it extra special, you could use tea bags to stain the map and tear the edges, to make it look like an ancient treasure map!

Parent/Carer tips

Label some of the key 'landmarks' in your garden to encourage your child to practise their reading.

SKILLS

☐ Language & communication	☐ Social skills	☐ Emotional regulation
☑ Literacy/Numeracy	☑ Problem-solving	☐ Sensory integration
☑ Concentration	☑ Motor skills	☑ Working memory

8. WATER GRAFFITI

Description
Children can develop their fine motor and gross motor skills with this relaxing, yet completely mess-free, activity!

Equipment
Water, plastic containers, paintbrushes and paving stones/concrete.

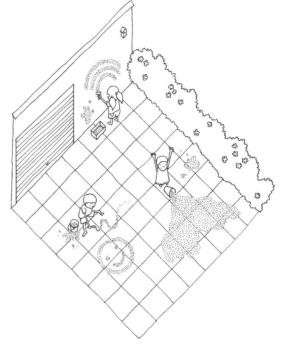

How to
1. Find a suitable area outside, such as paving stones.
2. Explain to your child that they have the rare opportunity to do some graffiti! They can paint as much as they like with water all over the paving stones!
3. Then let them watch how on a sunny day the sun will dry up their graffiti and make it 'disappear'.

Alternatives
Make footprints by filling a washing-up bowl with water and letting your child step in and out onto the paving stones.

Extras
Encourage your child to write letters, words and numbers to improve their letter and number formation as well as spelling.

Parent/Carer tips
As long as it wouldn't cause damage, your child could paint a wall or fence with water. Changing their position so they are painting an upright surface will encourage them to use their muscles in a different way, further helping to develop their motor skills.

SKILLS
☐ Language & communication	☐ Social skills	☐ Emotional regulation
☑ Literacy/Numeracy	☐ Problem-solving	☑ Sensory integration
☑ Concentration	☑ Motor skills	☐ Working memory

9. BAREFOOT SENSORY WALK

Description
A barefoot sensory walk can be wonderfully relaxing for children who love taking their socks off and getting messy!

Equipment
Trays/washing-up bowls, water, soil, sand, soap and leaves.

How to
1. Arrange trays/washing-up bowls around your garden, filled with different materials such as water, soapy water, sand and leaves.
2. If your child is willing, invite them to try stepping into each tray with bare feet, feeling the different textures.
3. Ask them to explain which is their favourite one and why.

Alternatives
If your child doesn't want to put their feet into the trays, ask if they'd like to touch them with their hands instead.

Extras
Make up a story with your child, pretending that each tray is a different place they have walked through. The sand could be a desert, the water a river, the leaves the forest floor, and so on.

Parent/Carer tips
Sensory activities like this one can help children who get overstimulated to feel more relaxed.

SKILLS

☑ Language & communication	☐ Social skills	☑ Emotional regulation
☐ Literacy/Numeracy	☐ Problem-solving	☑ Sensory integration
☐ Concentration	☑ Motor skills	☐ Working memory

10. BALLOON TENNIS

Description

Ball games can be tricky for children who are developing their coordination and gross motor skills. Balloon Tennis will not only make your children giggle, but as the balloons are big and slow, it's easier for children to succeed.

Equipment

Balloons and tennis rackets.

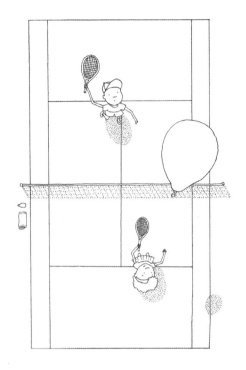

How to

1. Blow the balloon up to a large size.
2. Stand a couple of metres away from your child and encourage them to try to hit the balloon with their racket towards you.
3. Hit the balloon back to your child.

Alternatives

If you don't have a tennis racket you can use plastic fly swats or even just your hands (like volleyball).

Extras

This a great opportunity to sneak some maths into your play. Try counting how many times you can both hit the balloon.

Parent/Carer tips

This game can be challenging so encourage your child with praise and focus on the activity being fun, rather than their success at hitting the balloon each time.

SKILLS

☐ Language & communication	☑ Social skills	☐ Emotional regulation
☑ Literacy/Numeracy	☐ Problem-solving	☐ Sensory integration
☑ Concentration	☑ Motor skills	☐ Working memory

11. ANIMAL DEN

Description

Den building is great, but it can be time consuming. In my experience, it often ends up being made by the parents and not the child! This activity is just as fun but easier for children to make themselves.

Equipment

Twigs, leaves, pebbles, grass and leaves.

How to

1. Discuss what animals use for their den and why, thinking about their size, shape and how it would need to be waterproof and warm.
2. Provide them with materials you've chosen yourself or help them search in the garden for suitable materials to use.
3. Enjoy building a den together!

Alternative

Make a fairy house instead, using the same materials.

Extras

Choose the animal that you would like them to make the den for and give your child requirements for making the den, such as its size and shape.

Parent/Carer tips

Make sure the materials chosen from the garden are safe.

SKILLS

☑ Language & communication	☐ Social skills	☐ Emotional regulation
☑ Literacy/Numeracy	☑ Problem-solving	☐ Sensory integration
☑ Concentration	☑ Motor skills	☐ Working memory

12. TEDDY BEAR FESTIVAL

Description
Move over traditional teddy bear's picnics, we are having a teddy bear festival instead! Children can practise their social skills and communication, while enjoying some imaginative play in the garden.

Equipment
Teddy bears, a picnic rug, plastic plates, cups and a music player.

How to
1. Encourage your child to choose who has 'tickets' to their teddy bear festival; you could ask them why they have chosen certain teddies.
2. Plan the festival together. What music will you play? Will the teddy bears need to pretend to camp? What food should they bring?
3. Set up the festival and enjoy the sensory experience of listening to music while playing. Act out the teddies 'talking' to one another about the music and sharing a picnic.

Alternatives
Make a teddy bear birthday party instead!

Extras
Create a more realistic festival for the teddies, with tents to camp in, a cardboard box stage for the performers and even make paper wrist bands for the teddy bears to wear!

Parent/Carer tips
The aim is to encourage children to practise their social skills and communication. Try prompting your child to attempt conversations (if able to) between the teddies, or even model conversations yourself.

SKILLS

☑ Language & communication	☑ Social skills	☑ Emotional regulation
☐ Literacy/Numeracy	☐ Problem-solving	☑ Sensory integration
☐ Concentration	☐ Motor skills	☐ Working memory

13. WATER WALL

Description

Strategically attach plastic bottles to a wall/fence to create a lovely sensory water play activity. Children can pour water into the top one and watch it travel down the wall from one bottle to another.

Equipment

Plastic drinks bottles (empty and clean), scissors, heavy duty tape and a jug.

How to

1. The plastic bottles need to either be cut in half length ways, or have a section cut out of the top of them (by a responsible adult).
2. Using heavy duty tape, attach them to the wall/fence at slight angles, below one another to allow the water poured into the top bottle to travel all the way down to the bottom of the wall via each bottle. Make sure the top bottle is at an accessible height for your child.
3. Provide your child with a plastic jug to pour the water into the top bottle. Let them enjoy the sensory experience of hearing and watching the water travel down the wall.

Alternatives

Make this a more permanent feature by attaching the bottles using a drill to a board/sheet of wood. You could also use drainpipes.

Extras

Add food colouring or washing-up liquid to the water to make it even more visually stimulating.

Parent/Carer tips

Pouring water is great for hand–eye coordination and concentration. Ask your child how it makes them feel, helping them to associate sensory experiences with feelings of calm.

SKILLS

☐ Language & communication	☐ Social skills	☑ Emotional regulation
☐ Literacy/Numeracy	☑ Problem-solving	☑ Sensory integration
☐ Concentration	☑ Motor skills	☐ Working memory

14. PEBBLE PORTRAITS

Description
Children can get creative using pebbles and other bits and bobs from nature to create a picture of themselves. These pictures make a lovely and tactile keepsake.

Equipment
Pebbles, leaves, twigs, PVA glue and card.

How to
1. Make a picture of yourself outside using pebbles, leaves and twigs as an example for your child.
2. Encourage your child to choose some suitable items to create their own portrait. Prompt with questions about what they look like, what colour eyes they have, and so on.
3. Support your child, if needed, to stick the materials onto the card.

Alternatives
Your child can use the pebbles and leaves to create the letters of the alphabet or even words!

Extras
If your child has chosen to do a self-portrait, why not get a mirror or a photograph of them for extra support.

Parent/Carer tips
Modelling this activity can be really helpful for supporting working memory, especially if they find it difficult to organize the stages of a process to get to the end goal.

SKILLS

☐ Language & communication	☐ Social skills	☐ Emotional regulation
☐ Literacy/Numeracy	☑ Problem-solving	☐ Sensory integration
☑ Concentration	☑ Motor skills	☑ Working memory

15. MUD POTIONS

Description
A splash of water, a sprinkle of soil and a handful of leaves! How will you make your mud potions together? This activity embraces all the fun of the humble mud pies, but with the added bonus of a bit more structure and learning.

Equipment
Soil, water, plastic cups, plastic jug, plastic spoons, twigs, pebbles, grass and leaves.

How to
1. Provide various plastic containers, spoons and water.
2. Write down, or tell your child, the made-up recipe for their mud potions! It might be 'three small twigs, two pebbles, four spoonfuls of soil and five spoonfuls of water'.
3. Support them when finding and counting the ingredients. Discuss how the potion looks, feels and smells.

Alternatives
Let them choose their own ingredients and enjoy the freedom of pouring and mixing their potions.

Extras
Make labels to go on their finished potion and write down a recipe for a new potion together.

Parent/Carer tips
Choosing different sized plastic containers to pour into will add to the challenge, helping with their hand−eye coordination and motor skills.

SKILLS

☐ Language & communication	☐ Social skills	☐ Emotional regulation
☑ Literacy/Numeracy	☑ Problem-solving	☑ Sensory integration
☑ Concentration	☑ Motor skills	☑ Working memory

16. TOY SHADOW DRAWING

Description
Children can be fascinated by shadows and this activity is a great way of harnessing this interest to encourage them to put pen to paper.

Equipment
Plain paper, toys and pencils.

How to
1. Put a piece of paper on the floor (ideally a hard surface like concrete or paving stones) on a sunny day.
2. Position your child's toy(s) on the paper so that its shadow falls onto the paper.
3. Ask your child to draw around the shadow of their toy.

Alternatives
Instead of toys, children can draw around your shadow.

Extras
Draw around the shadow at different times of the day and discuss why the shadows have got bigger and smaller.

Parent/Carer tips
Drawing around shadows can be an exciting way to practise fine motor skills and drawing.

SKILLS
☐ Language & communication	☐ Social skills	☐ Emotional regulation
☐ Literacy/Numeracy	☐ Problem-solving	☑ Sensory integration
☑ Concentration	☑ Motor skills	☐ Working memory

17. MATHS HOP

Description

This is an active numeracy game that requires little more than some chalk. Children can practise recognizing basic sums while burning off some energy!

Equipment

Chalk and paving stones or concrete.

How to

1. Using chalk, draw out large circles onto paving stones or concrete. Inside each circle, write a number.
2. Start by calling out the numbers and asking your child to jump/hop onto the correct number.
3. Dependent on their ability, next call out sums such as '5 + 1' and ask them to jump/hop onto the answer circle.

Alternatives

Swap the numbers for letters of the alphabet and get them to spell a certain word by jumping from one letter to the next!

Extras

If your child is able to, they can take turns to shout out the instructions to practise their speech, language and communication skills.

Parent/Carer tips

Adapt this activity to suit your child's numeracy abilities, with the aim to build their confidence through play.

SKILLS

☑ Language & communication	☑ Social skills	☐ Emotional regulation
☑ Literacy/Numeracy	☐ Problem-solving	☐ Sensory integration
☑ Concentration	☑ Motor skills	☐ Working memory

CHAPTER 2

ON A WALK

18. REMOTE CONTROLLED ROBOT

Description
This is an entertaining activity where children can take turns being a robot who is 'controlled' by the remote. It is brilliant for learning to process and follow verbal instructions.

Equipment
Remote control (an old TV remote control or homemade from cardboard).

How to
1. Chat about what a robot is and what remote controls are used for. Explain that you will be pretending to direct them around the garden using the remote.
2. Press the buttons while shouting out the instructions; these may include 'go', 'stop', 'move forward two steps', 'jump forward with two feet' and 'turn around'.

Alternatives
This activity is designed for outside, but it can easily be done inside too.

Extras
Swap roles, with your child being in charge of giving out instructions. This will help them develop their confidence in their language and communication skills.

Parent/Carer tips
Practise physical skills such as jumping with two feet off the ground or hopping. Further develop their working memory by making the robot 'programmable', giving your child multiple instructions to remember and then carry out.

SKILLS

☑ Language & communication	☑ Social skills	☐ Emotional regulation
☑ Literacy/Numeracy	☐ Problem-solving	☐ Sensory integration
☑ Concentration	☑ Motor skills	☑ Working memory

19. SHAPE SEARCH

Description

It is amazing how many shapes you see on a walk, whether it be the rectangular doors on the square houses or the oval petals on a flower. Children will love searching for these shapes on their stroll.

Equipment

No equipment needed for this activity, just the opportunity to go on a family walk!

How to

1. Start by talking about the different shapes your child knows. This might be two-dimensional shapes such as circles, squares and triangles, or three-dimensional shapes such as spheres and cubes.
2. Point out different objects on your walk and discuss their shape. Examples include a square window on a house or maybe a circular road sign.
3. Encourage your child to take turns to point out shapes too.

Alternatives

Search for the letters of the alphabet instead (on road signs, postboxes etc.), to practise their literacy skills.

Extras

Make this more challenging by introducing more complex shapes such as hexagons and pentagons.

Parent/Carer tips

This activity can be as structured or as open-ended as you like. You may focus on one shape at a time, just looking for squares first, for example. Or you may decide it is more fun to shout out shapes as and when you all find them.

SKILLS

☑ Language & communication	☑ Social skills	☐ Emotional regulation
☑ Literacy/Numeracy	☐ Problem-solving	☐ Sensory integration
☑ Concentration	☑ Motor skills	☐ Working memory

20. TREE RUBBINGS

Description
Jump into nature with this enjoyable and sensory activity. It's fantastic for developing hand strength and fine motor skills while admiring the wonders of the natural world!

Equipment
Paper, pencil and a tree.

How to
1. Enjoy looking for suitable trees on your walk.
2. Encourage your child to hold the piece of paper against the tree with one hand and then using their pencil, colour in the sheet of paper.
3. Remove the paper from against the tree and ask them to describe how it looks.

Alternatives
You can rub coins or leaves.

Extras
Experiment with different coloured crayons. Your child could make a rainbow tree rubbing.

Parent/Carer tips
This activity is designed to try to help children's hand strength and fine motor skills. These skills can help improve children's handwriting and their stamina when writing.

SKILLS

☑ Language & communication	☐ Social skills	☐ Emotional regulation
☐ Literacy/Numeracy	☐ Problem-solving	☑ Sensory integration
☐ Concentration	☑ Motor skills	☐ Working memory

21. TEXTURES AND SOUNDS NATURE HUNT

Description
A mindful and relaxing nature hunt that requires children to use more of their senses, ideal for children who are feeling overstimulated.

Equipment
No equipment needed.

How to
1. On your walk, try to encourage your child to stop and listen for loud and quiet sounds.
2. Discuss if you can hear any high-pitched sounds or low rumbling sounds.
3. Next try to see if you can find anything rough, smooth, soft or hard.

Alternatives
You could listen for sounds at home or in the garden.

Extras
Record the bird sound that you hear using a mobile device or collect leaves with interesting textures to bring home. Make your own mindful book with some of the textured things you have found.

Parent/Carer tips
Being mindful and using more senses can help children to regulate their emotions. It's an important skill to model to children. You could discuss how they are feeling after the walk and ask if they feel calmer – this reinforces the benefits of such activities to them.

SKILLS

☑ Language & communication	☐ Social skills	☑ Emotional regulation
☐ Literacy/Numeracy	☐ Problem-solving	☑ Sensory integration
☑ Concentration	☐ Motor skills	☐ Working memory

22. COLLECT THE COLOURS

Description
Children love picking things up on walks, whether it be a stick or an interesting pebble! So why not embrace this hobby with this colourful activity.

Equipment
Card, coloured pencils and sticking tape.

How to
1. Divide a piece of A4-sized card into four sections using a ruler and pencil; colour the top of each section with a different colour.
2. Take the card with you on a walk, along with some sticking tape.
3. Ask your child to find something of each of the colours and to stick them to the matching coloured section.

Alternatives
Instead of colours, choose textures like 'rough', 'smooth', 'soft' or 'hard'.

Extras
Your child can use all the treasures they have collected to create a colourful collage.

Parent/Carer tips
This activity is great for developing working memory as it involves your child following a simple step-by-step sequence.

SKILLS
☐ Language & communication	☐ Social skills	☐ Emotional regulation
☐ Literacy/Numeracy	☑ Problem-solving	☐ Sensory integration
☑ Concentration	☐ Motor skills	☑ Working memory

23. LEAF TWIN

Description

This lovely nature challenge provides children with opportunities to develop problem-solving skills, as well as reinforce their understanding of sizes and shapes.

Equipment

Paper, pencils, ruler (optional extra) and sticky tack.

How to

1. Find a leaf on your walk with your child.
2. Place the leaf on a piece of paper and ask your child to try to draw around it.
3. For the rest of your walk, try to find leaves that match this leaf in size and shape (your leaf's twin!) by putting each leaf you find on top of your outline to see if it matches. Discuss sizes and shapes of the leaves.

Alternatives

This can be done with other objects from nature, such as stones and shells.

Extras

Take a ruler with you to measure the leaves, helping your child to develop their numeracy skills.

Parent/Carer tips

If your child finds it tricky drawing around the leaf while holding the paper still, you could temporarily stick it down using some sticky tack.

SKILLS

☐ Language & communication	☐ Social skills	☐ Emotional regulation
☑ Literacy/Numeracy	☑ Problem-solving	☐ Sensory integration
☑ Concentration	☑ Motor skills	☐ Working memory

24. ALL THE PHOTOS OF THE RAINBOW

Description

Take photographs together of things for each colour of the rainbow during your walk, documenting the red postbox, orange flowers and bright green grass!

Equipment

Camera or camera phone and a picture of a rainbow/ list of colours (optional).

How to

1. Chat with your child about the colours of the rainbow. You may decide to write them down or bring a picture of a rainbow with you to refer to on your walk.
2. Each time your child spots something of one of the colours of the rainbow, (if appropriate) encourage them to try to take a photograph of it.
3. When you return home, you could look through the photos you have taken together and put them in the order of the rainbow.

Alternatives

Set your family a rainbow daily challenge and focus on just one colour of the rainbow each day, getting family and friends involved in sharing their photos of that colour that day with you too!

Extras

Print the photos off to create a small scrapbook of your rainbow photos.

Parent/Carer tips

Taking photographs can be an accessible alternative to collecting objects for physically disabled children. If a child is colour-blind, you could adapt this to focus on the colours they can easily distinguish between.

SKILLS

☑ Language & communication	☐ Social skills	☐ Emotional regulation
☐ Literacy/Numeracy	☑ Problem-solving	☐ Sensory integration
☑ Concentration	☐ Motor skills	☐ Working memory

25. PLAY DOUGH IMPRINTS

Description

Find some of nature's treasures and squish them into some play dough to see their detailed imprints! It's a fabulous way of keeping children entertained during a walk!

Equipment

Play dough.

How to

1. Look for things like leaves, stones, sticks, pinecones and shells on your walk.
2. Discuss with your child any with interesting patterns or detail.
3. Press your 'finds' into some play dough to make an imprint!

Alternatives

Pick flowers and press them between paper instead.

Extras

Bring your finds home and press them into some salt dough. Then allow the salt dough to dry, leaving permanent imprints in the solid salt dough. See activity 82 for a salt dough recipe.

Parent/Carer tips

Taking imprints with play dough can be great for developing fine motor skills and hand strength (squishing and shaping the play dough).

SKILLS

☐ Language & communication	☐ Social skills	☐ Emotional regulation
☐ Literacy/Numeracy	☑ Problem-solving	☑ Sensory integration
☑ Concentration	☑ Motor skills	☐ Working memory

26. RANDOM DESTINATION

Description

Add some mystery to your walks by flipping a coin at each junction to determine which way to walk! Heads for right, tails for left – let the coin decide. This is fantastic for helping children learn their left from right –just make sure you know the way back home!

Equipment

A coin.

How to

1. On your walk, whenever you come to a suitable junction, ask your child to flip the coin, if they are able to.
2. If the coin lands on heads, then turn right. If the coin lands on tails, turn left.
3. After a little while, stop the game and find your way back home together.

Alternatives

If you don't have a coin with you, there are plenty of free apps on mobile devices that allow you to flip a virtual coin.

Extras

On your return, draw a map of where you went, labelling where you turned left and right, if you can remember.

Parent/Carer tips

The process of flipping the coin, working out if it's heads/tails and then remembering if that means you are going left or right is brilliant for developing working memory skills.

SKILLS

☑ Language & communication	☑ Social skills	☐ Emotional regulation
☐ Literacy/Numeracy	☑ Problem-solving	☐ Sensory integration
☐ Concentration	☐ Motor skills	☑ Working memory

27. JOURNEY COLLAGE

Description
Pick and stick to create a collage of your journey to illustrate to others the textures and colours on your walk.

Equipment
A bag (to carry things you collect), glue, paper, scissors and a pencil.

How to
1. During your walk, prompt your child to collect suitable objects they find on their journey.
2. On your return, open your bag and discuss together each object they found.
3. Support your child to cut and stick these objects on to a piece of paper to tell the story of their journey.

Alternatives
If collecting objects isn't suitable for your child, take photographs and print these to make the collage instead.

Extras
Help your child create a story board of their journey, sticking their objects in the correct order of when they found them.

Parent/Carer tips
Make sure your child doesn't pick up anything hazardous.

SKILLS

☑ Language & communication	☐ Social skills	☐ Emotional regulation
☐ Literacy/Numeracy	☑ Problem-solving	☐ Sensory integration
☐ Concentration	☐ Motor skills	☑ Working memory

28. SEASON HUNT

Description

Armed with a clipboard and pencil, your child will feel like a proper explorer for this nature hunt! Great for developing concentration skills, it couldn't be simpler to prepare.

Equipment

Paper, clipboard and a pencil.

How to

1. Have a chat about which season it is and what you might see on your walk. For example, in autumn you might see fallen leaves and people in coats.
2. Draw a simple tick chart of all the things you think you might see on your walk, using words or pictures.
3. Help your child to tick off the things they see on your walk.

Alternatives

If you don't have a clipboard, use a piece of card.

Extras

Your child could have a go at making their own tick sheets – drawing and writing the things to find!

Parent/Carer tips

Be in charge of the pencil yourself! Not only would it be massively disappointing if they lost their pencil mid-way through, but it can pose a risk to your child's safety if they are running with their pencil.

SKILLS

☑ Language & communication	☐ Social skills	☐ Emotional regulation
☑ Literacy/Numeracy	☑ Problem-solving	☐ Sensory integration
☑ Concentration	☑ Motor skills	☐ Working memory

29. NATURE CREATURES

Description
This activity will have your little ones chuckling away as they create creatures from the things they can find in nature. Trust me on this one, adding googly eyes to sticks, leaves and conkers is comedy gold for young children!

Equipment
PVA glue, googly eyes, paint (optional) and a bag.

How to
1. On your walk together, help your child to collect suitable objects from nature to make their creatures with. For example, these could be sticks, pebbles, leaves or pine cones. Put them in a bag to bring home.
2. Help them to stick the googly eyes to their sticks, stones or leaves with glue to create nature creatures!
3. They could add paint for further decoration.

Alternatives
Take the googly eyes with you on your walk and place (not stick) them temporarily on leaves that you see and take a photograph of them! Be sure to remove the googly eyes afterwards.

Extras
Why stop at *one* nature creature? Why not create a whole family of leaf or conker people? Your child could give them names, ages and even make up their hobbies.

Parent/Carer tips
As well as developing fine motor skills, this activity provides opportunities to develop a child's understanding of emotions. Encourage your child to draw sad, smiley or worried faces on their creatures and ask them why they might be feeling that way.

SKILLS
☑ Language & communication	☐ Social skills	☑ Emotional regulation
☐ Literacy/Numeracy	☐ Problem-solving	☐ Sensory integration
☑ Concentration	☑ Motor skills	☐ Working memory

30. BUG TALLY

Description

Wherever you go for your walk, you can almost guarantee that you will see some sort of mini-beast! Embrace this and use these bugs to help your child's numeracy skills in this fun task.

Equipment

Pen, paper and magnifying glass (optional).

How to

1. Before your adventure, have a think about the different types of mini-beasts you are likely to come across on your walk together.
2. Write/draw these mini-beasts in a list on a piece of paper, leaving space at the side for the tally.
3. On your walk, help your child to fill in the tally next to each mini-beast when they see it.

Alternatives

This can easily be done for other creatures, such as birds.

Extras

If your child finds the tally chart easy, create a graph of their results together to show which mini-beast was the most prevalent.

Parent/Carer tips

Tally charts can encourage children to put pen to paper while helping them develop their numeracy skills.

SKILLS

☐ Language & communication	☐ Social skills	☐ Emotional regulation
☑ Literacy/Numeracy	☐ Problem-solving	☐ Sensory integration
☑ Concentration	☑ Motor skills	☐ Working memory

31. PARKED CAR MATHS

Description

Those parked cars on your walk may never be seen as an eye-sore again, thanks to the opportunity they now provide to reinforce your child's addition and subtraction skills!

Equipment

Pen and paper (optional).

How to

1. When you spot a car registration plate, ask your child which numbers are on it.
2. Ask if they can add the numbers on the registration plate together, if they are able to.
3. If they find this easy, encourage them to then subtract the numbers away from one another.

Alternatives

If this is too challenging for your child, use it as a chance to practise number or letter recognition.

Extras

Set a family challenge to see who can find the car registration plate which will make the biggest number when you add the numbers together.

Parent/Carer tips

At all times, ensure that your child is under direct supervision and not near cars.

SKILLS

☑ Language & communication	☐ Social skills	☐ Emotional regulation
☑ Literacy/Numeracy	☑ Problem-solving	☐ Sensory integration
☑ Concentration	☐ Motor skills	☐ Working memory

32. STREET BINGO

Description

Make your walks competitive and exciting by creating your own bingo cards of things you may see or hear on your walk. Who will fill their bingo card first?

Equipment

Paper and pens.

How to

1. Draw a grid of six squares for each person.
2. Put pictures or words of the things you might see on a walk, one in each square. This will be specific to where you are going for your walk but may include 'person walking a dog' or 'bird tweeting', for example.
3. See who can fill their bingo card out first!

Alternatives

Street bingo doesn't have to be just for things you can see; depending on your child's needs, it can be for things you can hear instead.

Extras

Use words instead of pictures. Your child will have to read each of their six things instead of relying on the images.

Parent/Carer tips

It may be helpful to split up into teams, ensuring your child has sufficient support to spot/hear the things on their bingo card and cross them off.

SKILLS

☑ Language & communication	☑ Social skills	☐ Emotional regulation
☐ Literacy/Numeracy	☐ Problem-solving	☐ Sensory integration
☑ Concentration	☐ Motor skills	☐ Working memory

33. FOLLOW THE ADVENTURE MAP

Description

With a bit of planning and preparation, your normal walk around the block can be transformed into a fully fledged adventure, complete with map!

Equipment

Paper and pens.

How to

1. Draw a simple map of where you will be going. Include landmarks that your child may remember, such as the postbox and shop. Choose your destination, for example the sweet shop.
2. Explain to your child that they are going to be an explorer and will be using this map on their adventure!
3. On your walk together, help them use the map to work out the right way to go to get to their destination.

Alternatives

Write down 'sat nav' directions for your child. These are great for testing your child's ability to follow written instructions instead of visuals.

Extras

Get your child to draw their own map, either real or fictional.

Parent/Carer tips

Following a map is a great life skill; however, it can be tricky so keep it fun and lighthearted while providing lots of support.

SKILLS

☐ Language & communication	☐ Social skills	☐ Emotional regulation
☑ Literacy/Numeracy	☑ Problem-solving	☐ Sensory integration
☑ Concentration	☐ Motor skills	☑ Working memory

CHAPTER 3

SITTING STILL

34. PASTA TOWERS

Description

A simple, yet addictive, activity, this helps children develop their fine motor skills and concentration by carefully constructing pasta towers.

Equipment

Play dough/sticky tack, spaghetti and pasta tubes.

How to

1. Put a small amount of play dough on a table and then stick a piece of spaghetti upright into it, so that it stands up by itself on the table.
2. Ask your child to 'thread' the pasta tubes on to the spaghetti until they reach the top, counting as they go.
3. Children could race against you or a sibling to see how quickly they can put the tubes onto the spaghetti to reach the top without snapping the spaghetti in the process.

Alternatives

Plastic beads can be used instead of pasta tubes.

Extras

Create patterns using coloured pasta tubes.

Parent/Carer tips

Only encourage your child to race against siblings or the timer once they have mastered creating a tower themselves first. Competition can be good for learning important social skills, such as losing gracefully.

SKILLS

☐ Language & communication	☑ Social skills	☐ Emotional regulation
☑ Literacy/Numeracy	☐ Problem-solving	☐ Sensory integration
☑ Concentration	☑ Motor skills	☐ Working memory

35. CUPCAKE COUNTING

Description

Children will enjoy filling the cupcakes with pom poms to create their 'cakes'. You will love that they are practising a whole host of numeracy skills through play, including number recognition, counting, addition and subtraction.

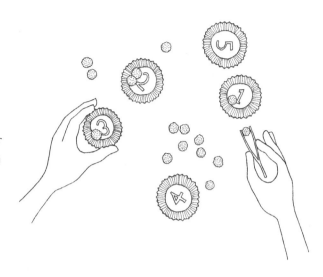

Equipment

Five cupcake cases, pens, pom poms, a bowl and plastic tweezers/scoops/spoons.

How to

1. Write a number from 1 to 5 in the base of each cupcake case.
2. Ask your child to read aloud the number in the cupcake case.
3. Encourage them to use their tweezers or scoop to put the correct number of pom poms into the cupcake case to make their 'cake'.

Alternatives

Although pom poms appeal because of their bright colours and fluffy texture, any small object can be used.

Extras

Practise subtraction and addition using the pom poms. For example, ask your child how many pom poms there would be if you subtract one from the cake.

Parent/Carer tips

This activity is not only brilliant for numeracy skills, it is also fantastic for fine motor skills and problem-solving.

SKILLS

☑ Language & communication	☐ Social skills	☐ Emotional regulation
☑ Literacy/Numeracy	☑ Problem-solving	☐ Sensory integration
☑ Concentration	☑ Motor skills	☐ Working memory

36. LETTER BUBBLE WRAP POP

Description
I've not yet met a child who doesn't gravitate towards a piece of bubble wrap! So why not harness this love of popping and sneak in some literacy practice too?

Equipment
Bubble wrap and a marker pen.

How to
1. Using the bubble wrap face up, write one letter of the alphabet on each bubble.
2. Once the marker pen has dried, call out a letter and ask your child to pop that letter.
3. You could extend this activity to ask your child to try to spell short words by popping the bubbles, for example 'cat'.

Alternatives
Use numbers, shapes or even colours on each of the bubbles.

Extras
Write some of the phonics digraphs on the bubbles instead, such as 'ch'.

Parent/Carer tips
Make sure your child is supervised with bubble wrap.

SKILLS

☑ Language & communication	☐ Social skills	☐ Emotional regulation
☑ Literacy/Numeracy	☐ Problem-solving	☑ Sensory integration
☐ Concentration	☑ Motor skills	☐ Working memory

37. CAFE SOUND SEARCH

Description
Sitting in a cafe or restaurant can be tough going for children. This game is great for keeping them occupied easily. You're simply encouraging your child to listen for key sounds to tick off on a piece of paper when they hear them.

Equipment
Paper and pens.

How to
1. Chat about all the noises you can hear. If you're in a cafe this may be things like a rumbling coffee machine, the clinking of cutlery, or two people having a conversation. Try to be very specific with your ideas.
2. Write them down on a list, with a tick box drawn next to each one. If your child needs visuals, use drawings instead of words.
3. Support your child in trying to listen for these sounds and then ticking them off when they hear them.

Alternatives
If your child is deaf or has a degree of hearing loss, this game can easily be adapted to ticking off the things they can see instead.

Extras
Make this game competitive by creating bingo grids with the sounds to cross off.

Parent/Carer tips
Listening out for sounds can sometimes help children who feel overwhelmed by an environment, allowing them to focus just on the sense of hearing. It may be beneficial, if they wanted to, to close their eyes.

SKILLS
☑ Language & communication   ☑ Social skills   ☑ Emotional regulation
☐ Literacy/Numeracy   ☐ Problem-solving   ☑ Sensory integration
☑ Concentration   ☑ Motor skills   ☐ Working memory

38. COIN TOWERS

Description

Who can build the tallest tower in the shortest time, using just coins? This is an exciting challenge that can be set up almost anywhere to keep children learning through play while sitting still!

Equipment

Selection of coins.

How to

1. Provide your child with various coins and show them how to balance one on top of another to make a tower.
2. Challenge them to build the tallest tower they can without it falling over.
3. Together, count the number of coins in their tallest tower.

Alternatives

If you don't have any loose change available, you can use coasters to build bridges and houses instead. Like coin towers, these also require hand–eye coordination and concentration.

Extras

Encourage them to build not just the tallest tower but the one with the highest monetary value – adding up the coin values as they build.

Parent/Carer tips

Balancing and positioning coins on top of one another is fantastic for concentration and fine motor skills. If your child is likely to put things in their mouth, then adapt this activity to use coasters as opposed to coins.

SKILLS

☐ Language & communication	☐ Social skills	☐ Emotional regulation
☑ Literacy/Numeracy	☐ Problem-solving	☐ Sensory integration
☑ Concentration	☑ Motor skills	☐ Working memory

39. ALPHABET BRICK MATCH

Description
Create your very own alphabet matching activity using building blocks, paper and pens!

Equipment
Plastic building blocks (that connect to each other), paper, pens and sticky tape.

How to
1. Write a few letters of the alphabet in upper- and lower-case on separate, small pieces of paper.
2. Tape them to plastic building blocks that can connect to one another.
3. When your child picks up a building block, if they are able to, ask them to read out the letter and then support them in finding the matching lower-case letter block to attach to it.

Alternatives
Instead of letters you can match numbers to their written form. For example, '1' to 'one'.

Extras
Practise spelling by connecting letters together to make words.

Parent/Carer tips
Physically connecting the upper- and lower-case letters together can help some children remember them more easily.

SKILLS

☑ Language & communication	☐ Social skills	☐ Emotional regulation
☑ Literacy/Numeracy	☑ Problem-solving	☐ Sensory integration
☐ Concentration	☑ Motor skills	☑ Working memory

40. SHAPE SPLAT

Description
A fast-paced game that helps children develop their knowledge of shape names by hitting them with the palm of their hand when they hear their name!

Equipment
Paper and pens.

How to
1. On a large piece of paper, draw out a selection of shapes.
2. Shout out the name of a shape, ask your child to find it and splat it with their hand.
3. Take it in turns to call out the shapes.

Alternatives
They can splat numbers, letters or words.

Extras
To make this activity even more fun, why not use plastic fly swats to splat the shapes with?

Parent/Carer tips
Processing verbal information can be tricky for some children, so give your child plenty of time to find the shape themselves, and provide prompts if necessary.

SKILLS

☑ Language & communication	☑ Social skills	☐ Emotional regulation
☑ Literacy/Numeracy	☐ Problem-solving	☐ Sensory integration
☑ Concentration	☑ Motor skills	☐ Working memory

41. DICE MATCH

Description
A simple, yet competitive dice game that helps children develop numeracy skills through play!

Equipment
Two dice, paper and pens.

How to
1. Jot the numbers 2–12 on a piece of paper.
2. Take it in turns to roll the dice, adding the numbers on the dice together.
3. Ask your child to tick off the number they make. Repeat until all the numbers have been ticked off.

Alternatives
Make this easier using just one dice and concentrating on the numbers 1–6.

Extras
If your child enjoys competition, have a separate sheet each and race each other to tick off all the numbers first!

Parent/Carer tips
It's almost inevitable that the dice will roll off the table. If you've got a bowl available, roll the dice in that instead to reduce this problem. Although competitive games can be problematic with children, learning how to be a good winner/loser can be an important social skill.

SKILLS

☑ Language & communication	☑ Social skills	☐ Emotional regulation
☑ Literacy/Numeracy	☐ Problem-solving	☐ Sensory integration
☐ Concentration	☐ Motor skills	☑ Working memory

42. MEMORY DRAW

Description
Now you see it, now you don't! Show your child an object, hide it and test their memory skills to draw what they saw. This is easy to play while out and about when sitting still.

Equipment
Paper, pencils and something to make a divider (book, magazine etc.).

How to
1. Choose an object on the table for your child to draw, discuss its shape and any key features.
2. Put a divider up so they can no longer see the object (this could be using a book on the table, or they could turn their chair the other way).
3. Ask them to try to draw the object from memory, then take down the barrier and see if it matches.

Alternatives
Instead of drawing, your child can explain how the object looks from memory. Or they can feel the object and describe how it feels.

Extras
Challenge your child to try to draw from memory something they have seen earlier in the day.

Parent/Carer tips
Have a go at this activity yourself, to help you see how tricky it can be. This will also help you to support your child when playing, giving them tips on how to memorize the object.

SKILLS

☐ Language & communication	☑ Social skills	☐ Emotional regulation
☐ Literacy/Numeracy	☐ Problem-solving	☐ Sensory integration
☑ Concentration	☑ Motor skills	☑ Working memory

43. MIRROR MIRROR

Description

This game involves your child having to try to mirror your actions. It is fantastic for developing a child's coordination and concentration.

Equipment

Mirror (optional extra).

How to

1. Sit your child so they are facing you. Explain that they have to pretend there is a mirror between the two of you and they must try to copy your movements.
2. Start with simple (one-step) movements such as putting your right hand in the air.
3. Try to encourage your child to copy a sequence of movements such as putting your right hand in the air, then on your head, then touch your nose.

Alternatives

Adapt this to copying sounds and noises.

Extras

You may want to support them with this activity by showing them their reflection in a mirror.

Parent/Carer tips

This activity requires a fair bit of processing. Children have to process what they can see you doing, work out the mirrored image of this (e.g. if your right arm moves, their left arm moves) and then physically move those muscles. It's a great activity for developing memory skills and concentration, especially if they are copying a sequence of movements.

SKILLS

☐ Language & communication	☑ Social skills	☐ Emotional regulation
☐ Literacy/Numeracy	☑ Problem-solving	☐ Sensory integration
☑ Concentration	☑ Motor skills	☑ Working memory

44. MUSICAL EMOTIONS

Description
Listening to music can be wonderfully therapeutic for so many children; it can change moods and provide calm. This activity reinforces the link between music and emotions, getting children to think about how the music makes them feel.

Equipment
Pens, paper and a music player/mobile phone (with a variety of music).

How to
1. Chat about music and how it can make us feel. Discuss the different types of emotions and draw simple faces (that depict emotions) on a piece of paper – for example, happy, sad, tired, excited and angry.
2. Play a short clip of some music to your child. Ask them to point to which emotion face it made them feel.
3. Repeat with another clip.

Alternatives
A simpler version is to listen to the music together and for you to point to the emotion yourself.

Extras
Your child can draw their own faces each time they listen to a clip, to show how it makes them feel. You could even ask them *why* the music made them feel this way.

Parent/Carer tips
Explaining and expressing feelings can be really challenging for children (and, let's face it, adults too). Persevere to help them to make the link between the music and their feelings.

SKILLS

☑ Language & communication	☐ Social skills	☑ Emotional regulation
☐ Literacy/Numeracy	☐ Problem-solving	☑ Sensory integration
☑ Concentration	☐ Motor skills	☐ Working memory

45. CRAFTY LETTERS

Description

Practising forming letters of the alphabet doesn't have to be restricted to pen and paper. In fact, for many children, creating the letters of the alphabet using different mediums can help them to remember the letter shapes more easily!

Equipment

Pen, paper, glue stick and different craft materials (e.g. pom poms, lollipop sticks, sequins and stickers).

How to

1. Choose a few letters to concentrate on. Draw large letters on a piece of paper.
2. Encourage your child to make the shape of the letters by sticking their craft supplies onto the outline. For example, they could make a sparkly letter 'A' by sticking individual sequins along the outline.

Alternatives

Use play dough to mould and shape into the letters.

Extras

Create digraphs, words or even sums!

Parent/Carer tips

Take photographs of their creations to display at home, to help your child remember letter formations.

SKILLS

☐ Language & communication	☐ Social skills	☐ Emotional regulation
☑ Literacy/Numeracy	☐ Problem-solving	☑ Sensory integration
☑ Concentration	☑ Motor skills	☐ Working memory

46. COLOUR POST

Description

A lovely little activity that you can easily put together beforehand and take out with you. Children will love posting the coloured lollipops into the correct hole and emptying them out again.

Equipment

Small cardboard box, coloured lollipop sticks, scissors and felt-tip pens.

How to

1. Before you go out, cut small holes in the top of a cardboard box (just large enough for a lollipop stick to fit through), then colour next to each hole. Make sure you can open the box to get the lollipop sticks out and that you have coloured lollipop sticks that match each coloured hole.
2. Give your child the selection of lollipop sticks and show them the colours on the top of the box. Prompt them to post the coloured lollipop stick into the matching coloured hole in the box.
3. Once all lollipops have been posted, open the box and start again!

Alternatives

Use pipe cleaners instead of lollipop sticks for an added fine motor challenge.

Extras

Use this to practise the alphabet by writing the letters of the alphabet on the lollipop sticks and on the holes.

Parent/Carer tips

Not only is this activity brilliant for practising colours, but picking up the lollipop sticks and posting them through the holes is a fun way to develop fine motor skills and hand–eye coordination.

SKILLS

☐ Language & communication	☐ Social skills	☐ Emotional regulation
☐ Literacy/Numeracy	☑ Problem-solving	☐ Sensory integration
☑ Concentration	☑ Motor skills	☐ Working memory

47. DRAW WHAT YOU FEEL

Description

Help your child to focus on the sense of touch, by asking them to draw what they can feel on paper as someone gently 'draws' on their back with their finger.

Equipment

Paper and pencils.

How to

1. With your finger, gently 'draw' a familiar shape on their back with your finger. Start with something simple, like a circle.
2. Ask your child to draw what they have felt onto the piece of paper.
3. Repeat this, each time making the shape more challenging.

Alternatives

Give verbal instructions of a shape for them to draw, allowing them to focus on their hearing as opposed to touch.

Extras

Try drawing the letters of the alphabet or numbers to help with their numeracy and literacy skills.

Parent/Carer tips

Focusing solely on one sense can help some children find calm when they are feeling overwhelmed. Ask your child if they would like to play this game – for some children it may not be very enjoyable, and they may prefer the verbal alternative.

SKILLS

☐ Language & communication	☑ Social skills	☑ Emotional regulation
☐ Literacy/Numeracy	☑ Problem-solving	☑ Sensory integration
☑ Concentration	☑ Motor skills	☐ Working memory

48. ALPHABET SPOT

Description
Use your surroundings to help keep your child entertained by spotting things that begin with certain letters of the alphabet and adding them to your diagram.

Equipment
Paper and a pencil.

How to
1. On a piece of paper, draw five large circles (with space around them) and in each write a different letter of the alphabet.
2. Look around with your child and see what you can spot that starts with each letter of the alphabet on your paper. For example, what can they spot that starts with the letter A?
3. Write the words of things you spot with that letter next to each letter circle on your page.

Alternatives
Instead of writing what they see, they can draw it. Or you can draw it for them.

Extras
Make this more challenging by using digraphs like 'sh' and 'ch' instead of letters, seeing what they can spot that has those digraphs in the word.

Parent/Carer tips
Work together as a team to complete this activity, helping your child to understand the important social skill of teamwork.

SKILLS

☑ Language & communication	☑ Social skills	☐ Emotional regulation
☑ Literacy/Numeracy	☑ Problem-solving	☐ Sensory integration
☐ Concentration	☑ Motor skills	☐ Working memory

49. CEREAL SORTING

Description
This yummy activity will keep your child well and truly occupied. While sorting activities can be wonderful for developing a child's fine motor control and concentration, they are often even better if food related!

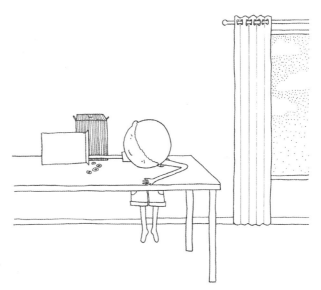

Equipment
Plastic bowls, a plastic plate, various types of small cereal and tweezers (optional extra).

How to
1. Empty different types of dry cereal onto a plastic plate. For example, cornflakes, cereal hoops and porridge oats.
2. Set up the table with plastic bowls (one for each type of cereal).
3. Model this activity by putting one of each of the cereals into a bowl. Encourage them to do the same, sorting the cereals into their types.

Alternatives
I chose cereals as they are usually quite a healthy choice, however, you may decide that sweets might make this a bit more enticing! You can also sort by colour, size or shape.

Extras
Using tweezers to pick up the cereal can make this activity fantastic for developing hand strength and fine motor control.

Parent/Carer tips
As with mealtimes, supervise your child and ensure that ingredients are checked for any relevant allergens.

SKILLS

☐ Language & communication	☐ Social skills	☐ Emotional regulation
☐ Literacy/Numeracy	☑ Problem-solving	☑ Sensory integration
☑ Concentration	☑ Motor skills	☐ Working memory

50. MEMORY MATCH

Description

This adaptable game is easy to make and great fun to play when your child needs to sit still. It is fabulous for practising children's memory skills through play too.

Equipment

Paper and pens.

How to

1. Divide and cut an A4 piece of paper into six. Draw a different shape on three of the pieces of paper and repeat on the remaining three (so that you have three pairs of shapes).
2. Place the pieces of paper face down on the table.
3. Support your child in choosing one of the pieces of paper and then trying to find (then remember) the matching shape.

Alternatives

To make this easier and more engaging, choose something your child is particularly interested in, such as drawings of superheroes or dinosaurs.

Extras

Try matching letters of the alphabet, numbers or even basic sums! You can also make this more difficult by using more squares of paper.

Parent/Carer tips

If your aim for this activity is to help develop their memory skills, then choose something simple to be drawn on the pieces of paper instead of making the subject complicated too.

SKILLS

☐ Language & communication	☐ Social skills	☐ Emotional regulation
☐ Literacy/Numeracy	☑ Problem-solving	☐ Sensory integration
☑ Concentration	☐ Motor skills	☑ Working memory

CHAPTER 4

RAINY DAY PLAY

51. SHAPE DETECTIVES

Description

Set your little detective the task of finding objects from around the house to match shapes you've drawn on a piece of paper.

Equipment

Paper, pens and various household objects.

How to

1. Draw a collection of shapes on a piece of paper.
2. Chat about different objects in the house and what shape they are. For example, the TV remote might be a rectangle and a coaster could be a square.
3. Explain to your child that you are both 'shape detectives' and your mission is to work as a team to try to find objects that match each of the shapes you've drawn out on the paper.

Alternatives

Instead of a 'shape detective', your child may prefer to be a 'colour detective' (finding objects of set colours) or an 'alphabet detective' (finding objects beginning with certain letters).

Extras

Make this more exciting by drawing around particular objects, instead of drawing set shapes, and encourage them to solve the mystery of which object you drew around!

Parent/Carer tips

This is a great opportunity to sneak some extra maths into their play. Look together at how many sides are on their shape and what other objects they could have found of that particular shape, for example.

SKILLS

☑ Language & communication	☑ Social skills	☐ Emotional regulation
☑ Literacy/Numeracy	☑ Problem-solving	☐ Sensory integration
☐ Concentration	☐ Motor skills	☐ Working memory

52. PLAY DOUGH BAKERY

Description

Let your child's pretend culinary skills come to life with this fun role-play activity! It's fantastic for fostering imagination and creativity, as well as developing fine motor skills.

Equipment

Play dough, bun cases and pom poms/sequins/beads (optional extras).

How to

1. Show your child a picture of a cupcake. Explain that you are going to pretend that the play dough is cake and create your very own play dough cupcakes. Remind your child that this is a pretend cupcake and it is not edible.*
2. Set out the various 'ingredients' in bowls and give your child a bun case.
3. Support your child as they roll and squish the play dough into the bun cases and choose their decorations (pom poms, sequins etc.) for toppings.

Alternatives

They could make pretend cakes, pies and croissants!

Extras

Write out a pretend 'recipe' for some buns. This could be as simple as three balls of play dough, two pom poms and five sequins (great for developing numeracy and reading skills).

Parent/Carer tips

*If your child is likely to put these in their mouth, swap the play dough and other materials for something edible.

SKILLS

☐ Language & communication	☐ Social skills	☐ Emotional regulation
☑ Literacy/Numeracy	☑ Problem-solving	☑ Sensory integration
☐ Concentration	☑ Motor skills	☐ Working memory

53. BISCUIT CONSTRUCTION SITE

Description
Have fun creating the yummiest of
building sites together, complete
with biscuit bricks and chocolate
cement! This is a brilliant sensory
play activity that's great for hand–
eye coordination and motor skills.

Equipment
Various biscuits, cereal, chocolate
spread/icing and a plastic plate.

How to
1. Teach your child all about building sites, what sort of things they might be
   constructing, and so on. Explain that they will be building a house.
2. Show them the various 'building materials' they have to use and support
   them in building their house using the biscuits for bricks and chocolate
   spread/icing as cement!

Alternatives
They could build bridges, roads and skyscrapers!

Extras
Test the strength of their builds, seeing how much weight their houses can hold.
Have a competition over who can make the strongest build.

Parent/Carer tip
As with all food-based activities, ensure that any relevant allergens are avoided
and your child is always supervised when eating.

SKILLS

☐ Language & communication	☐ Social skills	☐ Emotional regulation
☐ Literacy/Numeracy	☑ Problem-solving	☑ Sensory integration
☐ Concentration	☑ Motor skills	☐ Working memory

54. MASKING TAPE RACE TRACK

Description
You don't need fancy toys to have fun racing toy cars at home! Masking tape stuck down to a solid floor can make the perfect race track! Parent bonus: it's also very easy to tidy up afterwards!

Equipment
Toy cars, masking tape, scissors and a solid floor/tuff tray.

How to
1. Using masking tape on a solid floor (or a tuff tray), stick the tape in the shape of a race track, complete with starting grid, lanes and pits!
2. Choose some toy cars to race on the track and let your child enjoy racing the cars around their very own track.
3. If they are able to, encourage them to provide commentary of the race, practising their speech, language and communication skills.

Alternatives
Create a village with roads or an airport with masking tape runways!

Extras
Encourage them to film their races with a mobile phone, recording their commentary.

Parent/Carer tips
While this activity may just appear to be playing with toy cars, there are opportunities throughout for them to practise cutting skills, fine motor skills and communication skills.

SKILLS
- ☑ Language & communication
- ☐ Literacy/Numeracy
- ☑ Concentration
- ☐ Social skills
- ☑ Problem-solving
- ☑ Motor skills
- ☐ Emotional regulation
- ☐ Sensory integration
- ☐ Working memory

55. PIRATE SHADOW TELESCOPES

Description

Ahoy there! Make your very own pirate shadow 'telescopes' that (with a clever use of a bit of clingfilm, card and a torch!) project their pirate pictures on the wall!

Equipment

Kitchen roll tubes, clingfilm, sticking tape, card, scissors, pencils, glue and a torch.

How to

1. Draw a small pirate picture on some card (no bigger than half the size of the base of your tube).
2. Cut out the picture and stick it onto some clingfilm with glue. Position the clingfilm over one of the ends of the kitchen roll tube, so that your cardboard picture is in the centre.
3. In a dark room, shine a torch down the tube and look at the silhouette of the pirate picture on your wall!

Alternatives

If you don't have any kitchen roll tubes, you can make a small square frame using cardboard to position the clingfilm and picture on instead.

Extras

Cut and stick letters on the clingfilm at the end of the tube, or even words. Just make sure you stick them the right way up!

Parent/Carer tips

While making the tubes is fantastic for hand−eye coordination and fine motor skills, it is very fiddly! Ensure your child doesn't get too frustrated by providing suitable support.

SKILLS

☐ Language & communication	☐ Social skills	☐ Emotional regulation
☐ Literacy/Numeracy	☑ Problem-solving	☐ Sensory integration
☑ Concentration	☑ Motor skills	☐ Working memory

56. NAIL SALON

Description
Set up your very own, stylish nail salon, complete with cardboard nails to paint! Children will love asking their cardboard clients how they would like their nails painting today.

Equipment
Cardboard, pencils, paints, paintbrushes and sequins/glitter/plastic gems (optional extras).

How to
1. Assist your child to draw around their hands on the cardboard.
2. Support them to cut out the hands, then draw where the nails are.
3. Pretend to be at a nail salon, painting the nails on the cardboard hands with paint! Encourage them to pretend they work in a nail salon, asking their 'client' how they would like their nails today, thinking about colours, patterns and embellishments.

Alternatives
Why not draw around toes instead of hands, and practise pedicures!

Extras
Be a 'fussy client' giving specific details on how you would like your cardboard nails. Not only will this cause lots of giggles, but it's a great way of developing working memory – listening to your requests, remembering them and acting on them.

Parent/Carer tips
This activity can be fantastic for children who don't normally enjoy painting and colouring, as there's more structure to the task. Role-playing a nail salon is a great opportunity to practise language and communication skills.

SKILLS

☑ Language & communication	☑ Social skills	☐ Emotional regulation
☐ Literacy/Numeracy	☑ Problem-solving	☐ Sensory integration
☑ Concentration	☑ Motor skills	☐ Working memory

57. FROZEN SENSORY PLAY

Description
Create a realistic frozen landscape for any toy penguins and sea creatures, complete with icebergs and glaciers.

Equipment
Toy penguins/sea creatures, water, plastic cups, an ice cube tray, an oven tray, a tuff tray/washing-up bowl and blue food colouring (optional extra).

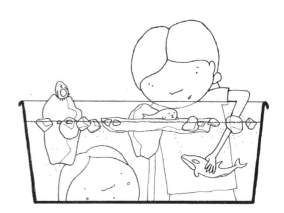

How to
1. Fill some plastic cups, ice cube tray and an oven tray with water. Leave in the freezer overnight.
2. Fill up a tuff tray/washing up bowl with water and add blue food colouring (optional extra). Take out the ice from the freezer. The ice in the plastic cups and ice cube trays can be icebergs of varying sizes. The ice in the oven tray can be glaciers or sheet ice. You may decide to break some of this up.
3. Let your child have fun adding sea creatures and role playing an imaginative, frozen world.

Alternatives
If your child isn't keen on the feel of ice, you can create an under the sea activity instead, just using the water and some toy sea creatures.

Extras
This activity provides a great opportunity to discuss climate change. Try adding slightly warmer water to see the effect it has on the 'glaciers' and icebergs.

Parent/Carer tips
If your child requires more structure for play, you could help to make up a story together of what's going to happen beforehand to help support their ideas. This could be, for example, 'the penguin jumps off the iceberg and swims underwater to find his friend'.

SKILLS

☑ Language & communication	☐ Social skills	☑ Emotional regulation
☐ Literacy/Numeracy	☐ Problem-solving	☑ Sensory integration
☐ Concentration	☑ Motor skills	☐ Working memory

58. AT THE GOLF COURSE

Description

Turn a cardboard box into your very own golf, target practice game! This is fabulous for gross motor skills and hand—eye coordination.

Equipment

Cardboard box, scissors, pen and a small soft ball.

How to

1. Cut out two holes in one side of your cardboard box (a suitable size so that the ball can fit through). Make sure the holes are right at the bottom of the box, so that the ball can roll in from the floor. Open the other side of the box, to allow you to get the ball out afterwards.
2. Demonstrate how to roll the ball across the floor to get it into the hole.
3. Take turns aiming the ball into one of the holes.

Alternatives

If you'd like to focus more on fine motor skills, do this activity using something small like marbles instead of a ball. Please note, marbles are a choking hazard.

Extras

Make this game educational by writing letters or numbers above each hole. Call out one of them and get your child to aim the ball into the correct hole!

Parent/Carer tips

You can make this activity more difficult by changing the size of the hole and the distance you aim from.

SKILLS

☐ Language & communication	☑ Social skills	☐ Emotional regulation
☐ Literacy/Numeracy	☑ Problem-solving	☐ Sensory integration
☑ Concentration	☑ Motor skills	☐ Working memory

59. DENTIST

Description

Learn all about the important role of a dentist with this hands-on, pretend teeth-brushing activity. Children will love scrubbing the pretend teeth to make them sparkling clean!

Equipment

Paper, sticky-backed plastic/file pockets/laminator, whiteboard pens and an old toothbrush.

How to

1. Print off or draw a picture of a smile with white teeth. Put it inside a see-through file pocket, or cover it in sticky-backed plastic, or laminate it.
2. Ask your child what they think happens to teeth after you eat something sweet. Draw with them, using the whiteboard pen, various plaque and food on the teeth.
3. Encourage your child to brush the teeth clean using the old toothbrush.

Alternatives

Instead of using a whiteboard pen, put shaving foam or chocolate spread on the picture to brush off!

Extras

Make this even more relevant to your child by using a photograph of *their* smile in the file pocket. Let them have a go at pretending to clean their own teeth!

Parent/Carer tips

You can also encourage speech, language and communication skills by getting them to 'act out' being the dentist.

SKILLS

☑ Language & communication	☑ Social skills	☐ Emotional regulation
☐ Literacy/Numeracy	☑ Problem-solving	☐ Sensory integration
☑ Concentration	☑ Motor skills	☐ Working memory

60. SWEET SHOP MATHS

Description
What better way to learn maths than to run your own pretend sweet shop! This is a very tempting way to engage children in learning how to count, add up and subtract.

Equipment
Various sweets, money and a toy till (optional extra).

How to
1. Put sweets in bowls on a little table in front of them, with their till or alternative. Write a price list together showing how much each sweet costs.
2. Pretend to be the customer asking for sweets and giving them the money.
3. Take turns being in charge of the till and being the customer.

Alternatives
If you want to avoid sweets this can be done with any suitable item that your child is interested in. It can be toys or even a juice stall (great for practising pouring!)

Extras
Why not take your sweet shop to the next level and make a sign, have shopping bags and write receipts!

Parent/Carer tips
This is a great activity for helping to develop speech, language and communication skills, especially if you act out being a very chatty customer!

SKILLS

☑ Language & communication	☑ Social skills	☐ Emotional regulation
☑ Literacy/Numeracy	☐ Problem-solving	☐ Sensory integration
☐ Concentration	☐ Motor skills	☑ Working memory

61. AVOCADO SAILORS

Description

If your child likes small-world play, they will love making their very own boats from an avocado and floating their 'sailor' (the stone) around a pretend sea!

Equipment

Avocado, knife (parent/carer only), spoon, tuff tray/washing-up bowl and acrylic paints (optional extra).

How to

1. Cut the avocado in half yourself (away from your child), keeping the knife out of reach.
2. Scoop out the centre of the avocado with a spoon. The avocado shell becomes the boat and the stone the sailor!
3. Fill a tuff tray/washing-up bowl with water. Pop the avocado on the water and put the little 'sailor stone' inside.
4. Encourage your child to play boats, sailing their avocado boat across the 'sea'.

Alternatives

Try other objects to see if they float – great for discussing the science of floating and sinking.

Extras

Why not paint the avocado stone to make it look like a sailor?

Parent/Carer tips

You could add food colouring or glitter to the water to make it even more of a sensory experience.

SKILLS

☑ Language & communication	☐ Social skills	☑ Emotional regulation
☐ Literacy/Numeracy	☑ Problem-solving	☑ Sensory integration
☐ Concentration	☐ Motor skills	☐ Working memory

62. POST OFFICE

Description
From weighing parcels to chatting to customers, there is so much for children to enjoy learning while running their very own post office!

Equipment
Kitchen scales, paper, stickers, envelopes, cardboard boxes, coins and a toy till (optional extra).

How to
1. Work with your child to set up their very own post office. Look at pictures or videos together of a post office and chat about what a post office is for. You may decide to sit your child at a table with the toy till and scales in front of them.
2. Pretend to be the customer with a parcel (cardboard box) or letter. Your child could weigh the parcel and tell you how much to pay and put stickers (pretend stamps!) on the parcels and letters.
3. Take it in turns to be the customer, practising speech, language and communication skills.

Alternatives
Write letters/addresses on envelopes and practise posting them into a pretend postbox (a cardboard box with a slit cut into it would work well).

Extras
Numeracy skills can be practised by handling money and weighing and writing down the weight of the parcels.

Parent/Carer tips
It is likely that a child will, as an adult, need to use a post office and therefore it's useful to learn how it works.

SKILLS

☑ Language & communication	☑ Social skills	☐ Emotional regulation
☑ Literacy/Numeracy	☐ Problem-solving	☐ Sensory integration
☐ Concentration	☐ Motor skills	☑ Working memory

63. CAR PARK MATCHING

Description

Tap into your child's love of cars to encourage them to learn upper- and lower-case letters in this enjoyable car parking game.

Equipment

Toy cars, paper, pens and sticking tape.

How to

1. Draw a car park on a piece of paper. Label each of the parking spaces with an upper-case letter.
2. Write the corresponding lower-case letters onto pieces of paper and stick them to the roofs of the toy cars.
3. Ask your child to try to park their toy cars in the matching letter spaces. This helps them to learn how to match upper-case and lower-case letters through play.

Alternatives

Write numbers on the car parking spaces and cars, getting your child to match numbers instead.

Extras

Write sums in the spaces and encourage your child to find the car with the answer on its roof to park in that space.

Parent/Carer tips

Using children's toys in learning can be a great way of engaging them in the task. Physically moving objects to answer a question can also help with information retention.

SKILLS

☑ Language & communication	☐ Social skills	☐ Emotional regulation
☑ Literacy/Numeracy	☑ Problem-solving	☐ Sensory integration
☐ Concentration	☑ Motor skills	☐ Working memory

64. PEPPERONI PIZZA MATHS

Description
Who knew pizza-making could be so mathematical? Tempt your children to practise some basic maths while imagining they are making scrumptious pizzas!

Equipment
Pens, paper, red coloured paper, glue and colouring crayons.

How to
1. Draw a circle the size of a dinner plate and split it into six sections. Write a number from 1 to 6 in each section, but don't repeat any numbers. Support your child in cutting out the circle and colouring it to make it look like a pizza.
2. Help your child to cut out small circles of red paper; these will be the pepperoni. You will need 21.
3. Ask your child to select a section/slice of the pizza, read the number on it and count that many 'pepperoni' pieces to go on it. Stick them down with glue. Continue with each of the slices until your pizza is complete!

Alternatives
If you are feeling brave (!) you can even have a go at doing this with a real pizza and real pepperoni, writing labels with the numbers on and placing them next to each slice.

Extras
Make it more challenging by writing sums on the slices. Children have to work out the answer to the sum on each slice, then find the correct number of pepperoni pieces and place them on the slice.

Parent/Carer tips
If picking up pieces of paper for the pepperoni is too fiddly, use balls of play dough instead. This activity is great for improving working memory as well as numeracy skills.

SKILLS

☐ Language & communication	☐ Social skills	☐ Emotional regulation
☑ Literacy/Numeracy	☑ Problem-solving	☐ Sensory integration
☐ Concentration	☑ Motor skills	☑ Working memory

65. CASH MACHINE

Description
A personal childhood favourite of mine, this game that requires little more than a cardboard box can amuse children for hours!

Equipment
Cardboard box, scissors, pens and pretend money (or paper).

How to
1. Look together at pictures of cash machines and try to turn your cardboard box into a replica.
2. Help the child to draw a screen on the front of the cardboard box, cutting slots using the scissors (responsible adult) for the card to go in and the money to come out. Draw the buttons and keypad. Make sure the box opens at the back for the person who is going to work the machine to access it.
3. Take it in turns to be the person using the cash machine, putting in your card, pin and withdrawing cash. Making sure to say out loud which buttons are being pressed so that the person behind it can give the correct money through the hole.

Alternatives
Depending on what would be useful for the child to learn, you may decide to change this to a ticket machine at a train station or a 'chip and pin' machine in a shop.

Extras
You could have an extra slot for receipts and practise writing receipts for withdrawals.

Parent/Carer tips
Using a cash machine is an important life skill. It may be helpful to write down or visually represent the stages of this process to start with – helping to improve their working memory.

SKILLS

☑ Language & communication	☑ Social skills	☐ Emotional regulation
☑ Literacy/Numeracy	☐ Problem-solving	☐ Sensory integration
☐ Concentration	☑ Motor skills	☑ Working memory

66. BEACH CLEAN-UP

Description
With plastic pollution hitting the headlines, this activity is not only wonderful and sensory, but also teaches children about the importance of keeping our beaches and seas clean of rubbish.

Equipment
Bucket, tweezers/tongs, sand, tuff tray/sand pit, plastic toys and anything else clean and safe that you can pretend is rubbish, and gloves (optional extra).

How to
1. Empty your sand into your tuff tray/sand pit. Put in various plastic toys and pretend rubbish.
2. Teach your child about plastic pollution and explain that litter on the beach can be dangerous to many animals that live on the beach and in the sea. Tell them that you are going to pretend this is a beach and your job is to pick up the litter and put it in the bucket.
3. Work as a team, putting on gloves and using tweezers or tongs to pick up the 'rubbish' from the sand and put in your bucket. This is a good way to practise sorting.

Alternatives
Do this on a smaller scale, putting the sand in a washing-up bowl or dinner tray.

Extras
Create miniature signs for your beach advising people not to throw litter.

Parent/Carer tips
Be mindful of what pretend rubbish you choose to put in the sand, making sure it's safe and doesn't have sharp edges.

SKILLS

☐ Language & communication	☑ Social skills	☐ Emotional regulation
☐ Literacy/Numeracy	☑ Problem-solving	☑ Sensory integration
☑ Concentration	☑ Motor skills	☐ Working memory

CHAPTER 5

CRAFTS

67. DOT TO DOT THREADING PLATE

Description

Threading activities are my secret weapon in developing fine motor skills and bilateral coordination. This activity not only achieves this, but children can also practise their numeracy skills in the process.

Equipment

Coloured wool, paper plates and a hole punch.

How to

1. Using the hole punch, make ten, evenly spaced holes around the outside of the plate, leaving a 1cm margin around the edge.
2. Next to each number write a random number from 1 to 10.
3. Tie a big knot in one end of the wool and support your child in threading the wool with their fingers through the 'number 1' hole to the 'number 2' hole and so on, until all ten have been done.

Alternatives

You can have letters of the alphabet written next to each hole for them to connect in order instead.

Extras

Use it as a way to practise maths sums by writing questions next to the holes on the left-hand side of the plate and the answers on the right-hand side. Ask your child to connect the question to its answer, by threading them together.

Parent/Carer tips

Although fiddly, this is brilliant for fine motor skills. Being able to do it themselves may also give them a huge amount of self-confidence and pride.

SKILLS

☐ Language & communication	☐ Social skills	☐ Emotional regulation
☑ Literacy/Numeracy	☑ Problem-solving	☐ Sensory integration
☑ Concentration	☑ Motor skills	☑ Working memory

68. PAPER CUP FRIENDS

Description
Make your very own people out of
paper cups and then use them as a
resource to help your child learn to
sort objects!

Equipment
Paper cups, googly eyes, PVA glue,
paints, scissors and sorting materials
(beads, coins, buttons etc.).

How to
1. Put the cups upside down on
   the table. Get your child to paint
   them and add googly eyes and other features. Cut out the mouth for them,
   ensuring it is big enough to fit the sorting materials in.
2. Choose your sorting material, for example buttons. Scribble a different colour
   on each one of the paper cup friends and put a selection of coloured buttons
   in front of your child.
3. Encourage them to feed the paper cup friends the correct coloured buttons.

Alternatives
If your child is likely to put the sorting materials in their mouth, adjust this
activity to sorting suitable food-based materials by size, colour and shape.
Always supervise your child around food.

Extras
Write numbers on small pieces of paper that will fit in their mouths and sort,
for example, odd numbers from even numbers.

Parent/Carer tips
Sorting activities are great for concentration and differentiating between
details.

SKILLS

☐ Language & communication	☐ Social skills	☐ Emotional regulation
☑ Literacy/Numeracy	☑ Problem-solving	☐ Sensory integration
☑ Concentration	☑ Motor skills	☐ Working memory

69. MELTED WAX CRAYON ART

Description

This is one of my favourite craft activities with children. It starts off being really messy and multicoloured, with bits of wax crayon everywhere and then with a quick bit of ironing (by a grown-up) it ends up being a beautiful piece of art!

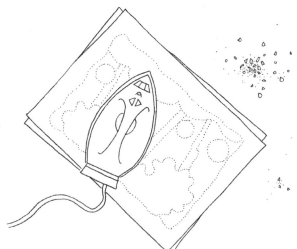

Equipment

Wax crayons, cheese grater, wax paper, paper and an iron.

How to

1. Before your child starts, grate different coloured wax crayons using a cheese grater.
2. Present your child with a piece of paper and the multicoloured grated wax crayons and ask them to create a picture (as abstract as they like!).
3. Once complete, with your child at a safe distance, put a piece of wax paper over the top of their creation and iron it gently on a low heat until it has melted onto the paper. Leave to completely cool before letting your child touch it.

Alternatives

Create sun catchers for the window by completing this activity on wax paper.

Extras

Give them a set picture to create, for example a rainbow.

Parent/Carer tips

Depending on your child's understanding of danger, you may choose to grate the wax crayons and iron the finished artwork when they aren't with you.

SKILLS

☐ Language & communication	☐ Social skills	☐ Emotional regulation
☐ Literacy/Numeracy	☐ Problem-solving	☑ Sensory integration
☑ Concentration	☑ Motor skills	☐ Working memory

70. BUBBLE WRAP PAINT SQUISH

Description
Combine the lovely sensory
properties of bubble wrap
with the squelching feeling of
squishing paint in this (almost)
mess-free activity!

Equipment
Bubble wrap, plain paper, coloured
paint and sticky tape.

How to
1. Put different coloured blobs of
   paint on the A4 piece of paper.
2. Create an envelope using the
   bubble wrap and pop the piece of paper inside, making sure the 'bubbles' face
   towards the paper.
3. Tape the edges down so that the paint stays inside then allow your child to
   stand on the bubble wrap in bare feet, squishing the paint below it onto the
   paper. Remove the paper from the bubble wrap envelope and leave to dry,
   admiring the patterned effect of the bubble wrap.

Alternatives
Paint the bubble wrap and then press it onto the paper. Bubble wrap makes a
lovely printing material.

Extras
When adding the paint to the paper, encourage your child to try to create a
picture and then observe how it changes after it's been squished!

Parent/Carer tips
This can be a relaxing sensory activity for children. Ensure your floors are
protected throughout.

SKILLS
- [ ] Language & communication
- [ ] Literacy/Numeracy
- [ ] Concentration
- [ ] Social skills
- [ ] Problem-solving
- [x] Motor skills
- [x] Emotional regulation
- [x] Sensory integration
- [ ] Working memory

71. BITS AND BOBS BRACELETS

Description
Arguably one of the easiest ways to make a bracelet with children! It's also a fantastically fiddly task for developing fine motor skills.

Equipment
Empty toilet roll tube, double-sided sticky tape and materials to stick onto it (e.g. sequins, glitter, beads, buttons).

How to
1. Set your child up with an array of the different equipment needed.
2. Help them to stick the tape to the outside of the empty toilet roll tube.
3. Encourage them to choose and stick various, different materials onto their bracelet until it is complete!

Alternatives
Instead of a bracelet, stick the tape onto some card and encourage them to create a picture with the materials.

Extras
Use this as a great opportunity to practise patterns, encouraging your child to position the beads/sequins in a set, repeating order.

Parent/Carer tips
What is great about the double-sided sticky tape is that children can do this activity reasonably independently as they don't need help gluing, which is great for their self-esteem.

SKILLS

☐ Language & communication	☐ Social skills	☑ Emotional regulation
☐ Literacy/Numeracy	☐ Problem-solving	☑ Sensory integration
☑ Concentration	☑ Motor skills	☐ Working memory

72. MARBLED ART

Description
When sensory play meets crafts! This mesmerizing activity can enable children to create the most beautiful pictures.

Equipment
Food colouring, water, thick paper, oil (cooking), a cake-cooling rack, a pipette, cocktail sticks and a baking tray.

How to
1. Half fill the baking tray with water and mix in some food colouring. Ask your child to use the pipette to suck up and squirt droplets of oil onto the top of the coloured water.
2. Use the cocktail sticks to move the blobs of oil around on top of the water.
3. Gently place the thick paper on top of the water, pull off and pop on a cooling rack to dry (put something underneath to protect your work surfaces). Once dry, chat about the beautiful patterns the oil created.

Alternatives
Instead of oil, you can use shaving foam. Squirt it onto the base of the baking tray and drop different colours of food colouring onto it, then as before, put the paper onto it and pull off and dry.

Extras
Experiment with changing the colours and the amount of oil to see how you can change the images created.

Parent/Carer tips
Remembering the order of the stages of this process can be good for helping children with their working memory. Initially, you may need to write the stages down or provide visuals to help them remember the order.

SKILLS

☐ Language & communication	☐ Social skills	☐ Emotional regulation
☐ Literacy/Numeracy	☐ Problem-solving	☑ Sensory integration
☑ Concentration	☑ Motor skills	☑ Working memory

73. STICKASAURUS SKELETONS

Description
Your child may have heard of a T-rex or a stegosaurus but probably not a 'stickasaurus'! Enjoy working together to create a made-up dinosaur skeleton using sticks.

Equipment
Sticks, PVA glue, paper and pencils.

How to
1. Collect sticks and twigs of varying sizes.
2. Look at some pictures of dinosaur skeletons in a book.
3. Draw an outline of the skeleton onto some paper and ask your child to stick the sticks onto the paper, pretending they are the dinosaur bones! Leave to dry.

Alternatives
Use uncooked spaghetti for the bones instead.

Extras
Instead of creating a two-dimensional dinosaur skeleton that is flat on the paper, try creating a three-dimensional one using plasticine to hold the sticks together!

Parent/Carer tips
The trickiest part of this craft activity is often that the sticks aren't the right shape and size – embrace this as is a way to develop their problem-solving skills.

SKILLS

☐ Language & communication	☑ Social skills	☐ Emotional regulation
☐ Literacy/Numeracy	☑ Problem-solving	☐ Sensory integration
☑ Concentration	☑ Motor skills	☐ Working memory

74. SHAPE ROBOT

Description
Follow instructions while learning and
manipulating shapes with this fun
robot craft! It's great for children who
prefer structured craft activities.

Equipment
Coloured card (cut into various
shapes such as squares, circles and
triangles), glue sticks, paper, pens
and googly eyes.

How to
1. Write out some robot making
   instructions, for example body
   made of three squares, circle for
   head and triangles for feet.
2. Help your child select the correct shapes.
3. Stick the shapes onto the paper to make the robot.

Alternatives
If your child is not yet able to read, you can verbally give them the instructions
or use pictures.

Extras
Add an extra level of difficulty by being specific in the instructions about which
colours you want for the robot.

Parent/Carer tips
Some children find open-ended crafts too daunting and don't enjoy them.
Although it might sound counterintuitive, adding structure like this can really
help to ignite a love of crafts.

SKILLS
☐ Language & communication ☐ Social skills   ☐ Emotional regulation
☑ Literacy/Numeracy   ☑ Problem-solving   ☐ Sensory integration
☑ Concentration   ☑ Motor skills   ☑ Working memory

75. TISSUE BOX HEDGEHOGS

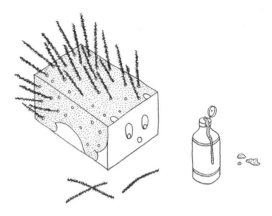

Description

Transform your empty, humble tissue box into a spiky hedgehog with this fine motor skill craft!

Equipment

Empty tissue box, pipe cleaners, pencils, pens, googly eyes, brown paint and paintbrushes.

How to

1. Support your child in painting the tissue box to look like a hedgehog (without the spikes). Stick googly eyes on the front and draw a nose and mouth.
2. Make lots of holes in the top of the box carefully, using a pencil (adult only).
3. Encourage your child to push pipe cleaners into the holes to create the spikes.

Alternatives

Make a hedgehog by using play dough and sticking the pipe cleaners into it.

Extras

Help your child to coil pipe cleaners around their finger, then pull off to make springs for the hedgehog's legs.

Parent/Carer tips

Posting the pipe cleaners through the holes is a fantastic way to help children with their hand–eye coordination and fine motor skills. To help with social skills, take turns to post the pipe cleaners.

SKILLS

☐ Language & communication	☑ Social skills	☐ Emotional regulation
☐ Literacy/Numeracy	☑ Problem-solving	☐ Sensory integration
☑ Concentration	☑ Motor skills	☐ Working memory

76. SPINNING SNAKES

Description

Children will love colouring and cutting out their very own spiralling, spinning snakes. And they will love them even more when they can watch them twirling from the ceiling!

Equipment

Paper, pens, scissors, colouring crayons, thread and sticky tack.

How to

1. Draw a spiral on a piece of paper with pen. Ask your child to colour in the spiral.
2. Provide them with some scissors so that, if they are able to, they can cut out their snake by cutting along the line as carefully as possible.
3. Open out the spiral snake, attach some thread to the head and stick it to your ceiling using sticky tack. Enjoy watching it spin and move!

Alternatives

If your child doesn't want to attach it to the ceiling, let them move around holding the thread attached to the snake instead! They can watch it follow them and wiggle in the breeze!

Extras

This activity can more challenging for cutting skills if you make the spiral tighter.

Parent/Carer tips

Cutting a spiral is no easy task as it requires children to move the paper around while they are cutting, which is great for developing coordination.

SKILLS

☐ Language & communication	☐ Social skills	☑ Emotional regulation
☐ Literacy/Numeracy	☑ Problem-solving	☑ Sensory integration
☑ Concentration	☑ Motor skills	☐ Working memory

77. TISSUE PAPER FLOWERS

Description

Create beautiful flowers out of tissue paper, dip them in food colouring, and enjoy watching the colour gently spread across the petals. A gorgeous, sensory craft.

Equipment

Tissue paper, parcel tape, scissors, food colouring, water and plastic cups.

How to

1. Support your child to twist the tissue paper until it is long and thin. Tape around three quarters of the length with parcel tape to make the stem.
2. To make the flower, cut downwards on the remaining quarter of tissue paper, towards the stem and open it out to form the petals.
3. Mix some food colouring with water in a plastic cup and ask your child to pop the flower into it, with just the bottom of the stem under the water. Watch the colour of the flower change as the coloured water travels to the flower up the stem. Leave to dry.

Alternatives

Use coffee filters instead of tissue paper.

Extras

Add some different coloured food colouring to parts of the petal before putting the whole flower into the water, giving the flowers multiple colours.

Parents/Carer tips

The parcel tape helps to make the stem look more realistic, but make sure you explain how the food colouring is still travelling up the stem. This activity can be calming as it requires children to sit still and concentrate on watching the colour seep into the petals.

SKILLS

☐ Language & communication	☐ Social skills	☑ Emotional regulation
☐ Literacy/Numeracy	☑ Problem-solving	☑ Sensory integration
☑ Concentration	☑ Motor skills	☐ Working memory

78. SENSORY NIGHT LIGHT

Description
Create a soothing, sensory, night light together. Who knows, it may have the added bonus of helping to make bedtimes easier!

Equipment
Clear jar, battery-powered tea lights, double-sided sticky tape and decorative materials (for example, sequins, coloured tissue paper, petals, leaves, twigs and shells).

How to
1. Discuss with your child the sorts of materials they find relaxing, thinking about colours and textures. Collect some of these decorative materials together, from the house or the garden, or on a walk.
2. Cover your clean jar/plastic cup with double-sided sticky tape.
3. Support your child in sticking various materials to the outside of the jar to create your nightlight. Put a battery-powered tea light (do not use a real candle as it would set fire) inside the jar and turn off the lights to look at it!

Alternatives
Create a calming collage, again letting them choose all their favourite materials and sticking them to a piece of paper.

Extras
Create shadows from the nightlight on the wall by using pieces of card cut out as shapes to stick to the outside of the nightlight.

Parent/Carer tips
Bedtimes and sleep can be really challenging for a lot of families, and while this probably won't be the magic answer, having ownership over something that is relaxing for bedtimes can only be a positive thing.

SKILLS

☐ Language & communication	☐ Social skills	☑ Emotional regulation
☐ Literacy/Numeracy	☑ Problem-solving	☑ Sensory integration
☑ Concentration	☑ Motor skills	☐ Working memory

79. SENSORY PRE-WRITING SHAPES

Description

Before learning to write the letters of the alphabet, it's important that children can practise pre-writing shapes. These are the shapes that they need to be able to make first in order to form letters. This educational craft idea helps children create their own sensory way of forming pre-writing shapes.

Equipment

Card, pipe cleaners, pencils and PVA glue.

How to

1. Support your child in cutting out squares of cardboard, about 10cm x 10cm.
2. On each square, help them to write a pre-writing shape. These include horizontal and vertical lines, circles, squares, crosses, x shapes, triangles and diagonal lines.
3. Choose a card and encourage your child to try to shape a pipe cleaner into the shape and stick it onto the outline. Repeat with the other cards and letters.

Alternatives

Instead of pipe cleaners, use play dough, sequins, beads or pom poms.

Extras

Once your child has mastered pre-writing shapes, repeat this activity to learn letters.

Parent/Carer tips

What's great about this activity is that your child creates a resource that they can refer back to.

SKILLS

☐ Language & communication	☐ Social skills	☐ Emotional regulation
☑ Literacy/Numeracy	☑ Problem-solving	☑ Sensory integration
☑ Concentration	☑ Motor skills	☐ Working memory

80. PLAY DOUGH MONSTERS

Description
Squish, roll and manipulate play
dough to create your very own
play dough monsters. This is
amazing for developing fine motor
skills, hand strength and creativity.

Equipment
Play dough, googly eyes, pipe
cleaners, lollipop sticks and sequins.

How to
1. Set your child up with some play dough and materials to add to it (googly
   eyes, pipe cleaners, lollipop sticks and sequins).
2. Show your child pictures of monsters in stories and talk about creating their
   own one with play dough.
3. Give them the freedom to try to create their very own monster themselves,
   if they are able to.

Alternatives
Be guided by your child's interests. Instead of a monster, it could be an alien or
an animal.

Extras
Develop speech, language and communication skills by asking them to describe
the features of their monster.

Parent/Carer tips
If your child needs a bit more structure for this activity, you could split this task
into stages. For example, roll a ball of play dough for the head, make a rectangle
for the body and add eyes to the face.

SKILLS

☐ Language & communication	☐ Social skills	☐ Emotional regulation
☐ Literacy/Numeracy	☑ Problem-solving	☑ Sensory integration
☑ Concentration	☑ Motor skills	☐ Working memory

81. EGG-BOX CATERPILLAR

Descriptions
Who knew that empty egg boxes make the perfect caterpillars? Just cut them in half, add some paint and a few bits and bobs and 'ta dah', your caterpillar is complete!

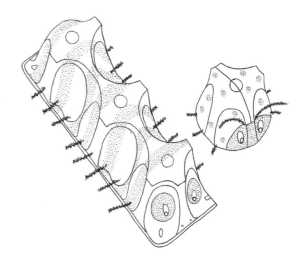

Equipment
Empty egg box, paint, paintbrushes, scissors, glue, googly eyes, pipe cleaners, buttons and lollipop sticks.

How to
1. Before your child starts making this, cut the egg box in half, lengthways and keep one half.
2. Turn it upside down so the dimples of the egg box are sticking upwards to make the segments of the caterpillar. Show your child pictures or videos of a caterpillar, and discuss the colours and features.
3. Provide them with their craft materials to paint the egg box and add googly eyes, pipe cleaner antennae and lollipop sticks for legs. Leave to dry.

Alternatives
Make this craft simpler by cutting out a single dimple from the egg box to decorate as a ladybird.

Extras
Extend this activity, if your child is able to, by asking them to write about mini-beast describing its features.

Parent/Carer tips
Children can really utilize their problem-solving skills during this task, working out how to turn their egg box into a caterpillar.

SKILLS

☐ Language & communication	☐ Social skills	☐ Emotional regulation
☐ Literacy/Numeracy	☑ Problem-solving	☐ Sensory integration
☑ Concentration	☑ Motor skills	☐ Working memory

82. SALT DOUGH FOSSILS AND FOOTPRINTS

Description
Making salt dough is one of my favourite things to do with children. It's surprisingly easy to make and just the right amount of messy to make it fun! This activity enables children to make imprints of toys, creating solid 'fossils' and footprints.

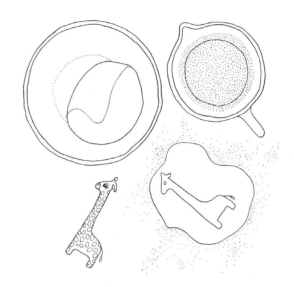

Equipment
Three-quarters of a cup of water, one cup of table salt, two cups of flour, a bowl, a mixing spoon and plastic toys.

How to
1. Together with your child, mix the water, salt and flour in a bowl. Take out of the bowl, place on a floured surface and knead.
2. Split the dough into several hand-sized balls. Choose a plastic toy, for example a dinosaur, push the toy into the salt dough and remove to make an imprint. If you press the body into it, it creates a 'fossil'. If your child would prefer to make footprints, they can press the toy's feet into it.
3. Leave to dry, either overnight air drying or in an oven for an hour or so at a very low temperature (checking regularly until hard).

Alternatives
Make their own handprints or footprints in the salt dough! Squishing their hands or feet into the dough can be great for children who enjoy sensory stimulation.

Extras
Once dry, paint them to make them look realistic.

Parent/Carer tips
It might help to use visuals to help your child understand the stages of making the salt dough. Learning the steps of an activity can be great for developing working memory.

SKILLS

☐ Language & communication	☐ Social skills	☐ Emotional regulation
☐ Literacy/Numeracy	☑ Problem-solving	☑ Sensory integration
☐ Concentration	☑ Motor skills	☑ Working memory

83. PINE CONE FACES

Description
Bring nature to life with this charming craft which has the added benefit of helping children understand their own emotions and those of others.

Equipment
Pine cones, googly eyes, paint, paintbrushes and PVA glue.

How to
1. Chat with your child about emotions and feelings, asking them questions such as, 'How can we tell if someone is happy?'. You may choose to support them with simple drawings of faces showing different emotions.
2. Collect pine cones. Paint them together and add googly eyes to make them look like people!
3. Encourage your child to decide how each pine cone is feeling, getting them to paint on their expression with a paintbrush. For example, a smile or a frown.

Alternatives
Use sticks, stones or leaves instead of pine cones.

Extras
Extend their understanding of emotions by asking them why their pine cones are feeling that way – help them to make up a pretend back story!

Parent/Carer tips
In my experience, kids find googly eyes on natural objects very funny, so embrace this and use it as your 'way in' to keep them engaged in the activity.

SKILLS

☑ Language & communication	☑ Social skills	☑ Emotional regulation
☐ Literacy/Numeracy	☐ Problem-solving	☐ Sensory integration
☐ Concentration	☑ Motor skills	☐ Working memory

CHAPTER 6

SENSORY PLAY

84. MINI-LIGHTBOX MESSY PLAY

Description
Lightboxes can be super for sensory play, but they are often costly and bulky. Therefore, try making your own mini-version! A delightful activity for emotional regulation.

Equipment
Two plastic containers/transparent sandwich boxes, flour, heavy-duty tape and a torch/battery-powered tea lights.

How to
1. Turn one of the plastic containers upside-down to make the stand and use the heavy-duty tape to tape over the sides. Put the battery powered tea light underneath this container. Tape another transparent box onto the top of this stand, keeping the tape on the sides only.
2. Part fill the plastic containers on the top with flour, and turn the torch/tea lights underneath on.
3. Let your child play with the flour, watching the way the light shines through into the top plastic container.

Alternatives
Replace the flour with any messy play ingredient, such as sand or cocoa powder.

Extras
Once you've made this lightbox, you can use it to do all sorts of activities. For example, you could use it as a way to practise their letter formation, drawing letters in the flour with their finger.

Parent/Carer tips
This can help some children to relax after a busy day or before bedtime. Always use battery-powered tea lights/torch rather than a real candle. Ensure that they don't overheat and that your child can't access their batteries.

SKILLS
☐ Language & communication	☐ Social skills	☑ Emotional regulation
☑ Literacy/Numeracy	☐ Problem-solving	☑ Sensory integration
☐ Concentration	☑ Motor skills	☐ Working memory

85. FROZEN FLOWERS

Description

This has to be the most captivating activity in the book. Collect flowers with your child, freeze them in ice cube trays with water and, once frozen, let your child enjoy playing with them on a tray. Ice play can be very therapeutic.

Equipment

Flowers, water, jug, ice cube tray, food colouring, glitter (optional extras) and a tray.

How to

1. Pick flowers together in your garden (or somewhere else with permission) and put them in ice cube trays.
2. Support your child to pour water into the tray, and then freeze it overnight.
3. Empty them out onto the tray and let your child enjoy playing with them.

Alternatives

While flowers are particularly stunning frozen in ice, you could easily swap them for other things you find on your walk, such as interesting leaves, twigs or pine cones.

Extras

To make it more visually stimulating, add food colouring and glitter to the ice cube trays.

Parent/Carer tips

Ensure that the flowers are safe for your child to touch. This activity isn't suitable for your child if they are likely to put the ice cubes in their mouth.

SKILLS

☑ Language & communication	☐ Social skills	☑ Emotional regulation
☐ Literacy/Numeracy	☐ Problem-solving	☑ Sensory integration
☐ Concentration	☑ Motor skills	☐ Working memory

86. RAIN MAKER TUBES

Description

This activity enables children to make their very own rain maker tubes, which make lovely gentle sounds. It is ideal for children who feel overstimulated.

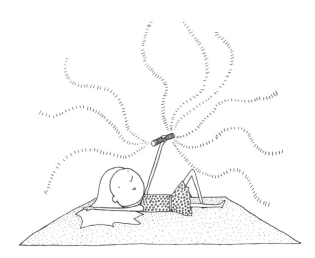

Equipment

Kitchen roll tubes, kitchen foil, clingfilm, sand, pom poms, beads, sticking tape, paints and paintbrushes (optional extras).

How to

1. Help your child to stick kitchen foil over one end of the kitchen roll tube.
2. Let your child choose various materials they would like to fill their tube with, discussing what sounds the soft and hard materials might make.
3. Once filled, tape the top of the tube with clingfilm. Encourage them to enjoy tipping it up and down, listening to the sounds it makes.

Alternatives

If your child prefers visual sensory stimulation to auditory or is deaf or has a degree of hearing loss, use an empty see-through bottle (instead of the kitchen roll tube), enabling them to see what's happening inside the tube!

Extras

To give your child more ownership over their rain maker, let them paint the outside of it.

Parent/Carer tips

The process of making these can help children develop their working memory, as they have to remember the stages involved. You may choose to support your child with visuals of the instructions.

SKILLS

☐ Language & communication	☐ Social skills	☑ Emotional regulation
☐ Literacy/Numeracy	☑ Problem-solving	☑ Sensory integration
☑ Concentration	☑ Motor skills	☑ Working memory

87. NATURE SUN CATCHER

Description
Transform your child's view through the window by creating these natural sun catchers. This simple craft showcases their discoveries from nature and provides visual, sensory stimulation.

Equipment
Paper plate, transparent/semi-transparent sticky-backed plastic, scissors, flowers, twigs, leaves and sticky tape.

How to
1. Help your child to cut out the centre of the paper plate. Put the sticky-backed plastic in its place and secure with sticky tape on the back.
2. Encourage your child to collect interesting things from nature to display on the sun catcher. This could be petals, twigs, leaves etc.
3. Stick these onto the sticky-backed plastic part of the sun catcher. Display on your window.

Alternatives
If you don't have sticky-backed plastic, use clingfilm and stick the objects on with PVA glue.

Extras
Instead of just cutting the central circle out of the paper plate, draw a shape or a letter to cut out instead.

Parent/Carer tips
Try to steer your child to choose translucent objects for their sun catcher, as that will allow the light to shine through.

SKILLS

☐ Language & communication	☐ Social skills	☐ Emotional regulation
☐ Literacy/Numeracy	☐ Problem-solving	☑ Sensory integration
☑ Concentration	☑ Motor skills	☐ Working memory

88. SOLID OR LIQUID?

Description
Mixing water and cornflour together creates a tactile, sensory play resource which seems to bridge the gap between solids and liquids! Pick it up in a solid ball then let go to let it drip back into the tray – incredible!

Equipment
Four-and-a-half cups of cornflour, two cups of water and a bowl/tray.

How to
1. In a bowl, with your child, mix the corn-flour and water until you get a sticky substance that can clump up like a solid, but then drips like a liquid.
2. Allow your child to put their hands in this and play.
3. Try hiding toys at the bottom of the tray for them to 'rescue'!

Alternatives
If you're feeling adventurous, why not take the tray outside and allow them to stand in it barefoot?

Extras
Put cocoa powder into the mixture to change the colour and smell, adding to the sensory experience.

Parent/Carer tips
While it's tempting to set these things up beforehand, making this sensory play resource together is all part of the fun, and it also enables children to use their problem-solving skills.

SKILLS

☐ Language & communication	☐ Social skills	☑ Emotional regulation
☐ Literacy/Numeracy	☑ Problem-solving	☑ Sensory integration
☐ Concentration	☑ Motor skills	☐ Working memory

89. DINOSAUR ICE EXCAVATION

Description
An exciting sensory activity for children, this is messy, fun and captures the interest of budding palaeontologists. Children will relish the opportunity to use basic science to excavate the dinosaurs from ice.

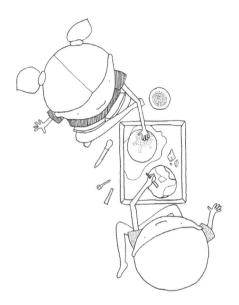

Equipment
Balloons, water, freezer, small toy dinosaurs, tray/tuff tray, warm water, a bowl, pipettes, salt, plastic tweezers, glue spatulas and plastic spoons.

How to
1. Stretch the balloons by blowing them up and then deflating them. Put one small dinosaur toy in each balloon, fill the balloon with water and put in the freezer overnight.
2. Open the balloons and put the frozen moulds onto a tray with a selection of 'excavation' equipment.
3. Work as a team with your child to excavate the dinosaurs from the ice. Try sprinkling salt on the ice, dropping warm water on them from pipettes and even chipping away at the ice using spatulas and spoons.

Alternatives
Freeze a few toys in a tray of water to create 'sheets' of ice to recreate the layers of rock.

Extras
Try putting food colouring into the water.

Parent/Carer tips
This is a great activity for problem-solving! Working as a team will also help with the social skill of teamwork.

SKILLS

☐ Language & communication	☐ Social skills	☑ Emotional regulation
☐ Literacy/Numeracy	☑ Problem-solving	☑ Sensory integration
☑ Concentration	☑ Motor skills	☐ Working memory

90. COCOA STENCILS

Description

Your house will smell delicious as you make these chocolate powder stencil pictures. It's a fantastic way of adding structure to sensory play, while creating gorgeous art work.

Equipment

Card, white paper, pencil, scissors, a tray, cocoa powder and a sieve/flour shaker.

How to

1. Help your child to choose a picture they would like as their stencil. Support them in drawing it on the card.
2. Get your child to cut out the stencil using scissors, if they are able to do so.
3. Put the stencil on a piece of white paper in the tray and help your child to sprinkle the cocoa powder over their stencil using the sieve. Once complete, gently remove the stencil to see the picture!

Alternatives

Instead of cocoa powder, use flour over black paper.

Extras

Encourage them to do stencils of letters or numbers.

Parent/Carer tips

If your child wants to 'keep' their pictures, take photographs of them and print them off.

SKILLS

☐ Language & communication	☐ Social skills	☑ Emotional regulation
☑ Literacy/Numeracy	☑ Problem-solving	☑ Sensory integration
☑ Concentration	☑ Motor skills	☐ Working memory

91. POTATO MASHER PAINTING

Description
The name of this activity says it all, and while it might sound like an unlikely painting implement, a potato masher may well be the future of mark-making!

Equipment
Paint, a potato masher, paper, paintbrushes (optional extra) and plastic bowls.

How to
1. Pour different coloured paints into separate plastic bowls.
2. Demonstrate putting the potato masher in a bowl of paint and then onto the paper, making a lovely pattern.
3. Let your child have a turn.

Alternatives
Lots of kitchen implements, for example forks and spatulas, make interesting patterns when used like this.

Extras
Use a paintbrush to paint directly onto the base of the potato masher. You could even help your child to make a rainbow print!

Parent/Carer tips
Embrace the mess this activity creates and just ensure that your work surfaces are protected. Messy play can be very therapeutic for children and help with their emotional regulation.

SKILLS
☐ Language & communication	☐ Social skills	☑ Emotional regulation
☐ Literacy/Numeracy	☐ Problem-solving	☑ Sensory integration
☑ Concentration	☑ Motor skills	☐ Working memory

92. RAINBOW RICE

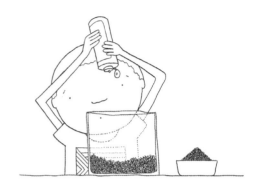

Description
Children can submerge themselves in the sensory experience of pouring, moving and playing with the most colourful of messy play materials.

Equipment
Uncooked rice, paint, sandwich bags, a tray, plastic spoons, plastic cups, plastic bowls and a plastic jug.

How to
1. Put a handful of rice into sandwich bags and add a dollop of paint. Close the bag and squeeze until the paint has covered each grain of rice.
2. Empty out onto a tray and leave to dry. Repeat with the other colours.
3. Put the coloured rice on a tray with the rest of the equipment (spoons, cups, jugs etc.) and allow your child to play at pouring, mixing and feeling the coloured rice.

Alternatives
If you don't have any paint, playing with dry rice in a tray can still be a lovely sensory experience for children.

Extras
If your child enjoys sorting activities, try mixing the rice up and asking them to play at sorting them into colours. This is fantastic for developing their pincer grip and colour recognition.

Parent/Carer tips
This activity isn't suitable if your child is likely to put the rice in their mouth; you could use cereal instead (without paint).

SKILLS

☐ Language & communication	☐ Social skills	☑ Emotional regulation
☐ Literacy/Numeracy	☐ Problem-solving	☑ Sensory integration
☐ Concentration	☑ Motor skills	☐ Working memory

93. PAINTING LETTERS ON ICE

Description
Learning how to form the letters of
the alphabet has never been so cool!
This freezing cold activity is much
more tempting than pen and paper!

Equipment
A transparent plastic container, water,
paint, paintbrushes, paper, pens and
salt (optional extra).

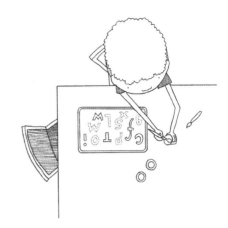

How to
1. Fill the container a quarter full of water and freeze overnight to create
   an ice sheet.
2. Write letters of the alphabet onto a piece of paper and put under the tray.
3. Support your child in looking through the ice to see the letters and trying
   to paint them on the ice above.

Alternatives
Instead of letters try numbers, words or anything else your child is working on.

Extras
Experiment with warm water and salty water, seeing if they melt the ice.

Parent/Carer tips
If your child needs support, paint on the ice yourself first and encourage them
to paint over your letters in a different colour.

SKILLS

☐ Language & communication	☐ Social skills	☐ Emotional regulation
☑ Literacy/Numeracy	☐ Problem-solving	☑ Sensory integration
☑ Concentration	☑ Motor skills	☐ Working memory

94. COLOURFUL SPAGHETTI SNAKES

Description

Love slime? Try making your very own, slimy, colourful slimy snakes by adding just a bit of vegetable oil and paint to some spaghetti!

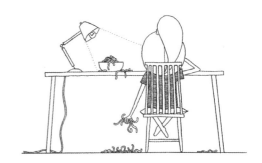

Equipment

Cooked spaghetti, vegetable oil, food colouring, water, tray and plastic scissors (optional extra).

How to

1. Take out a handful of spaghetti, add vegetable oil then food colouring and leave to dry. Repeat with the other colours until you have an array of different coloured spaghetti.
2. Put the spaghetti on a tray and let your child enjoy playing with it.

Alternatives

Use different types of cooked pasta to add different textures and shapes.

Extras

Use this as an opportunity to practise cutting skills by providing your child with some plastic scissors to cut the spaghetti.

Parent/Carer tips

Make sure you fully coat the cooked spaghetti in vegetable oil before adding the food colouring so that it sticks on the spaghetti. Also, be aware that this resource won't keep.

SKILLS

☐ Language & communication	☐ Social skills	☑ Emotional regulation
☐ Literacy/Numeracy	☐ Problem-solving	☑ Sensory integration
☐ Concentration	☑ Motor skills	☐ Working memory

95. JELLY RESCUE

Description
Get messy and sticky rescuing toys from the bottom of a bowl of jelly. It's lots of fun and great for problem-solving and hand–eye coordination.

Equipment
Jelly, water, a jug, clean plastic toys, bowl, fridge, spoons and spatulas (optional extras).

How to
1. Make the jelly in a bowl following the instructions on the packet, and add clean plastic toys to the bottom of the bowl before putting in the fridge to set.
2. Tell your child that they are going to pretend to be a Jelly Rescuer! Their job is to use their tools (spoons, spatulas and hands) to carefully rescue their toys.
3. Let your child enjoy feeling for and pulling out their toys from the sticky jelly!

Alternatives
To make the whole of this activity edible, try hiding sweets instead of toys to rescue!

Extras
If they are happy to do this, the child can do this activity with their eyes closed so they just have to use their touch sense to feel for the toys.

Parent/Carer tips
Using their pincer grip to pull out the toys from the jelly is great for fine motor skills.

SKILLS

☐ Language & communication	☐ Social skills	☐ Emotional regulation
☐ Literacy/Numeracy	☑ Problem-solving	☑ Sensory integration
☐ Concentration	☑ Motor skills	☐ Working memory

96. WHOSE FOOTPRINT IS IT?

Description

A footprint mystery for your children using paint and plastic toys. Get them using their problem-solving skills to work out whose footprint it is!

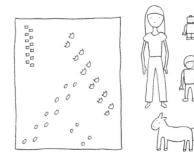

Equipment

Plastic toys, paint, paper and plastic bowls.

How to

1. Protect your surfaces and then put some paint into plastic bowls. Choose a handful of plastic toys that have feet.
2. Without your child seeing, choose one of the toys, dip its feet into the paint and press onto a piece of paper. Show your child the picture and get them to guess which toy made this footprint.
3. Take turns with your child to put the feet of each plastic toy into the paint and then press onto the paper, seeing which one matches the original footprint!

Alternatives

If your child doesn't want paint on their toys, you could use wet sand to press the feet of the toys into and then try to match the footprint.

Extras

This could make a lovely literacy activity, writing about whose footprint it was and how they worked this out.

Parent/Carer tips

Choose a paint that can be washed off the toys easily, and wash them soon after they have been used.

SKILLS

☑ Language & communication	☑ Social skills	☐ Emotional regulation
☐ Literacy/Numeracy	☑ Problem-solving	☑ Sensory integration
☑ Concentration	☑ Motor skills	☐ Working memory

97. CEREAL WORLD

Description
Picture this, a cereal landscape…
rolling hills of cornflakes, cereal hoop
grasslands and porridge mountains!
Create your very own small world using
dried cereals, perfect to set up in a tray
for children to play with their toys in.
They'll love the crunching sound when
their toys walk across the cereal terrain.

Equipment
Tray/tuff tray, various dry cereals and
plastic toys (animals, dinosaurs and people).

How to
1. Decide on a landscape – will it be a beach, mountains or desert? Select
   various different dried cereals and pour them into the tray to create the
   landscape. It works best if you have a few different ones next to one another.
   For example, you could have a desert using porridge oats next to a mountain
   of cornflakes or a muddy field of a chocolate cereal.
2. Choose some suitable toys for this environment.
3. Play with your child, acting out conversations between the various toys as
   they play in their landscape.

Alternatives
Instead of cereals, you can use dried pasta shapes, couscous and cocoa powder.

Extras
For added sensory stimulation, try adding an area of water in your landscape
(be prepared for mess!). You could also create a more realistic sand by using a
blender on some of the cereals.

Parent/Carer tips
Dried cereals can make a great alternative to sand play. Not only are they edible,
but their smells can also add to the experience.

SKILLS
☑ Language & communication   ☑ Social skills   ☑ Emotional regulation
☐ Literacy/Numeracy   ☐ Problem-solving   ☑ Sensory integration
☐ Concentration   ☐ Motor skills   ☐ Working memory

98. MUSICAL COLOURS

Description

Get musical and create your very own musical instruments using glass jars and coloured water! Sensory play is about sounds too!

Equipment

Water, a jug, three different coloured food colourings, three empty glass jars and a spoon.

How to

1. Support your child in pouring water into the three empty glass jars. Help them fill them to different levels: a quarter, a half and three-quarters full.
2. Encourage them to add a few drops of food colouring to each jar, so you have three jars of different coloured water and different levels.
3. Using the spoon, gently tap it against each jar and listen to the different sounds.

Alternatives

Try filling the last jar completely full of water and see if it changes the sound it makes when hit.

Extras

Can they make a tune using the jars?

Parent/Carer tips

Take care with the glass jars and supervise throughout in case of breakages.

SKILLS

☑ Language & communication	☑ Social skills	☑ Emotional regulation
☐ Literacy/Numeracy	☐ Problem-solving	☑ Sensory integration
☑ Concentration	☐ Motor skills	☐ Working memory

99. RAINBOW ICE TOWERS

Description
Attempt to build a slippy, frozen tower together with colourful ice blocks and then watch as it melts and mixes the colours together.

Equipment
Ice cube tray, water, food colouring and a tray.

How to
1. Pour water into an ice cube tray and add different colours of food colouring to each ice cube well. Leave to freeze overnight.
2. Empty the ice cubes out onto a tray, show your child a picture of a rainbow and look together at the order of the colours. Encourage your child to build a tower with their ice cubes in the same order as the rainbow.
3. Discuss why the ice is melting and what is happening to the colours as they mix.

Alternatives
Draw a tower of coloured blocks on a piece of paper (e.g. a tower of red, green, blue). Show your child the picture and ask them to copy it using their coloured ice cubes.

Extras
Try mixing primary colours to make secondary colours, by putting primary colours together and watching them melt and mix.

Parent/Carer tips
Ordering and balancing the ice cubes in the same order of the rainbow is not only challenging from a fine motor skills point of view, but it is also tricky for working memory.

SKILLS

☐ Language & communication	☐ Social skills	☐ Emotional regulation
☑ Literacy/Numeracy	☑ Problem-solving	☑ Sensory integration
☑ Concentration	☑ Motor skills	☑ Working memory

100. GLITTER BOTTLES

Description

Work together adding glitter, oil and water to a bottle to make a mesmerizing, sensory resource that children can use to help them feel calm.

Equipment

Glitter, beads, sequins, water, plastic bottles, heavy-duty tape, vegetable oil and food colouring (optional extra).

How to

1. Fill a clean, empty plastic bottle with water. Support your child in adding vegetable oil and food colouring.
2. Show your child various options of items they can add to their glitter bottle; this could be beads, glitter and sequins, for example. Let your child add them to the bottle.
3. Screw on the lid, and secure with heavy-duty tape. Let them enjoy tipping it upside down and watching the sequins and glitter rise and fall.

Alternatives

Use a bowl instead of a bottle and let them mix it then watch the sequins and glitter settle, before doing it again.

Extras

Help your child to associate watching this with a feeling of calm (if that's how it makes them feel), building their emotional regulation skills.

Parent/Carer tips

Make sure the lid of the bottle cannot be opened by your child in case of accidental ingestion, and supervise them throughout the activity.

SKILLS

☐ Language & communication	☐ Social skills	☑ Emotional regulation
☐ Literacy/Numeracy	☐ Problem-solving	☑ Sensory integration
☑ Concentration	☑ Motor skills	☐ Working memory

INDEX

· · · · · · · · · · · · · ·